CONSCIOUS BRAVERY:
Caring for Someone with Addiction

Pamela Brinker

CONSCIOUS BRAVERY

Caring for Someone with Addiction

Printed and Electronic Versions
ISBN 978-1-956353-20-4
ISBN eBook 978-1-956353-21-1
(Pamela W. Brinker/Motivation Champs)

The book was printed
in the United States of America.

Special discount may apply on bulk quantities.
Please contact Motivation Champs Publishing to order.
www.motivationchamps.com

ENDORSEMENTS

In *Conscious Bravery*, Pamela Brinker offers parents and loved ones compassionate guidance to meet the heroic tasks of supporting someone with addiction with greater courage and confidence. In her warmth, humanity, and storytelling, loved ones will find themselves in her pages. From the practical to the spiritual, her book offers comfort and insight to all who care about someone with addiction and mental health challenges. She calls readers to action, into the tasks of awareness, effective self-care, personal development, and guidance. I can think of no greater gift for those who are struggling to help than the clarity that comes out of the practices Pamela offers within the pages of *Conscious Bravery*.

—*Brad M. Reedy, PhD*
Author, Podcast Host, and Evoke Therapy Programs
Executive Clinical Director

Who needs this book? This book is for everyone who has ever struggled or failed in life. I guess that includes most people. In *Conscious Bravery*, Pamela Brinker thoughtfully guides you through a comprehensive examination of true bravery. We are living through a time of great change. Pamela has provided plenty of ideas and tips which will help us reevaluate how we manage our personal and professional life with courage and bravery. Her approach is straightforward and from the heart. Inspiring and insightful, Pamela's *Conscious Bravery* is a must have. Five stars!

—*Sejal Thakkar, TEDx Speaker*
Sejal Thakkar is on a mission to educate and empower people to create a world where everyone is treated with dignity and respect. She is responsible for cultivating a people-first culture at Nobody Studios. Sejal is a former employment law attorney.

Conscious Bravery is an important book for anyone faced with adversity and great challenges to read. With motivating teachings and reminders, Pamela calls loved ones of those with addiction and mental health challenges into the grit and grace of everyday training in bravery and long-term endurance which ultimately results from perseverance. Pamela writes a great deal from the firsthand life experiences that she has personally endured. This book is transformative, and there is nothing like it. Courage is a must in succeeding in life, and what *Conscious Bravery* offers is groundbreaking.

—*Steve Fraser*
1984 Olympic Champion, Greco–Roman Wrestling
National Olympic Coach of 2007 World Team Champions

Pamela writes an amazing book about self-discovery and the journey how to be brave in the face of personal tragedy and calamity, something we all understand and can experience. I love how she tells her stories, sharing her personal experience, then gives us a very practical methodology and how to use what she's describing. To me that's really the best part is being able to take this and put it back into my life and a functional way. I have enjoyed getting to know Pamela, and I think one of the most amazing things about her is her own journey of self-discovery and bravery, and it definitely comes through in her writing. I look forward to her next book and following her through her life adventures. I'm honored to be her friend and colleague.

—*Kevin Petersen, LMFT*
Founder of the Chronic Hope Institute

Pamela Brinker walks beside us as someone who knows how afraid we are to be alone in our human experience. Her living wisdom flows naturally through every sentence as she validates and normalizes the burning away of the layers of personality, which we bravely built to protect ourselves from suffering. More of an intimate soul friend than guide, she shows us the way of transmuting and opening through the pain, the confusion, and the hurt as we learn how to let go of the known for the unknown. I will be eagerly sharing this book with my friends and with my clients.

—*Bryan Maynard, M. Div., MA, LPC-MHSP*
Certified Sensorimotor Psychotherapist and Consultant

Conscious Bravery by Pamela Brinker addresses the everyday bravery we all need in order to navigate this roller coaster called life. It's not "if" a situation will arise when this conscious bravery is needed, but when. Brinker not only identifies the bravery that lies deep within each of us, she provides a very specific road map to tap into this amazing superpower that we all possess. In the hyperspeed of our modern world, so many of us try to outrun, stifle, or deny the many challenges that life is sure to serve up. Brinker explains that the only true way to face life's challenges is head on. Her honest accounts of her own challenges in life are a refreshing reminder that vulnerability is a necessary part of every person's journey toward bravery. *Conscious Bravery* seems to speak directly to my personal journey over the past decade of slowing down, rather than speeding up. Being comfortable with quiet, rather than surrounding myself with more noise. Looking within myself for the answers, rather than looking out. Throughout my acting and athletic careers, I wasn't ready to take on this journey, but I'm so glad I was finally able to enjoy the inner peace and serenity that comes with finding my everyday conscious bravery. Brinker's work is sure to serve as a helping hand in other people's personal journeys, if they are brave enough to take the first step and open her book.

—Hillary Wolf Saba
1996 & 2000 US Judo Olympian
Played Macauley Culkin's sister in "Home Alone" & "Home Alone 2"
Star of "Big Girls Don't Cry"

Pamela Brinker is a deeply thoughtful, creative, and compassionate human whose wisdom and insights come from years of practice of finding joy in difficult places and cultivating the courage and mindfulness to persevere. Her first book, *Conscious Bravery: Caring for Someone with Addiction*, is a toolkit for navigating through the hardest struggles we all face, with lessons drawn not just from her years as a practicing psychotherapist and clinical social worker, but from her experiences as a mother, partner, athlete, student, and a practitioner of mindfulness traditions. At the same time that it encourages us with insights about vulnerability, guarding our happiness, and returning to the breath as a daily practice, *Conscious Bravery* spurs our imaginations with her poignant storytelling. For many, this book will provide an anchor on which to rely when the winds are at their strongest, and the mountain seems too steep to take one more step. As someone who has been blessed to witness Pamela's path over the course of many decades, her honesty, vulnerability, and generosity are a source of hope while they simultaneously challenge me to find my own courage to live a life that embraces change, creativity and authenticity.

—Darrell Grant, Jazz Artist/Composer, Director,
The Artist as Citizen Initiative
Educator and Advocate for the Arts
11 Albums, including "Truth and Reconciliation," and "Black Art"

Pamela Brinker's book, *Conscious Bravery*, is an engagingly written revelation of vulnerability and bravery. The perspective is often in the first person which brings you into the heart, mind, and breath of the author. The reader is invited to imagine the colorful tapestry woven by the author which serves to allow active participation. In almost cinematic style stories, we, the audience, can witness the content in action. The chapters also include helpful exercises gently suggested to the reader. Pamela Brinker has shared a sensitive and heartfelt experience to the reader by bravely jumping into the pages without making a splash. I highly recommend this book to anyone interested in learning more about bravery, breath, and emotions.

—Ashok Bhattacharya is a psychiatrist, musician, artist, and author.
www.empathyclinic.com
YouTube: Dr. Ashok Bhattacharya
LinkedIn: Ashok Bhattacharya

At first glance, it would seem that *Conscious Bravery* is indeed a guidebook for those who care for others suffering from addiction; but, after delving more deeply into the pages of this tenderly nuanced volume, I soon realized that this poignant, vulnerable, and heartfelt book is more broadly relevant. Actually, it will benefit anyone striving both to become the best of who they are and to offer the best of who they are to those about whom they care. This unpretentious and understated gem of a book by Pamela Brinker features finely honed pearls of wisdom — "befriend your feelings, become comfortable with discomfort, breathe consciously, and know that you are your essence"— that are at once simple but profound, humble but sophisticated, unassuming but quietly compelling, and subtle but absolutely riveting. The richly textured tapestry that Pamela so lovingly weaves for the reader has, as its centerpiece, the importance of healing from the inside out—relevant for both caregiver and addict. Pamela's own awe-inspiring story is one of courageous action, gracious tenacity, passionate commitment, and awe-inspiring triumph in the face of shattering losses, devastating disappointments, and heartbreak. But throughout the pages of this compassionate and hope-infused chronicling of her sons' and her own healing journeys, Pamela's bravery, faith, and resilience shine through brilliantly—to illuminate the path for all those struggling to find their way out of the wilderness. Cherish this uplifting volume, relax into its gentle flow, and you will be able to feel that you are not alone.

—*Martha Stark, MD, Faculty, Harvard Medical School*
Award-winning Author: 9 Books on the Theory and Practice of Psychodynamic Psychotherapy, including Relentless Hope: The Refusal to Grieve

WOW—what a magnificent book on love, life, and bravery! Pamela is an exceptional teacher who combines life experience with her life's work. She's the one to teach us how to be brave through excruciating challenges because she's needed to be brave, herself. Through the pages she gently holds the reader's hand and offers actionable tools and examples so we can all show up at our bravest best, even when we think we can't. Anyone who reads this book and follows Pamela's lead will flourish.

—*Michele Waters, M.A.*
Dancing with the Diagnosis: Steps for Taking the Lead When Facing Cancer

Contents

To my two beloved sons
toiling on
through the wilderness.
Keep journeying!
I love you more than G.L.A.
You are my sunshines.
We are on this train, bound for Glory.

FOREWORD

If you or someone you love has been touched by addiction, or if you're just interested in this fascinating subject, I cannot recommend *Conscious Bravery* enough. This book contains a wealth of information about what it is to be brave, to make conscious choices, and about the emotional effects addiction has on us all. The reader will learn how to flourish as a loved one of someone who is suffering from addiction and the mental health challenges accompanying it. Mostly you will discover hope and faith! Pamela Brinker presents it in an organized manner while writing in a clear, beautiful, and understandable voice. Trust me; you will learn how to brave the wilderness of addiction and come out feeling supported and empowered. You will grow and learn about your soul.

Recovery from addiction is possible for our loved ones. Having a steady and dependable voice like Pamela's as a guide on this roller coaster of a journey is a gift, and I know how confusing, lonely, and heartbreaking it can feel to watch the people we love suffer. We have to take care of ourselves first and learn how to embrace conscious bravery.

Pamela Brinker is the voice we have all been looking for to take our hand and lead us to a safe place! Her book is a loving resource showing us how to find our own bravery and put it into action. Everybody who cares for someone touched by addiction needs direction walking alongside their loved one on this precarious journey. In these pages you will find specific concepts and techniques to help assist you in every step along the way.

Supporting anyone with addiction and/or mental health challenges requires adapting to an ever-evolving climate. Pamela's mission here is to help you find conscious bravery and apply it on your way through the changing unknown. This book promotes addiction and mental health awareness with new perspective for all who care to make a difference.

Conscious Bravery is a must read for anyone who is looking for support and wants to learn new ways of thinking and tools to survive and thrive! I hope this book reaches as many people as possible, since it contains such valuable content on an incredibly important topic. Everybody knows someone with either addiction or mental health issues, and *Conscious Bravery* speaks powerfully to all.

—*Erica Spiegelman, CADAC-II, author of Rewired: A Bold New Approach to Addiction and Recovery and The Rewired Life: Creating a Better Life Through Self-Care and Emotional Awareness*

ACKNOWLEDGMENTS

I am so grateful for you, dear reader, for coming along on this journey with me into the wilderness we didn't choose. I believe in you and have faith in your process. You can and will cultivate your bravery.

For everyone who has generously given their time, positivity, and ideas, walking beside me with this book: Keri, for your unceasing love and brilliance since before forever, Mer-sista; Emily, for your soul friendship, visionary organization, and our belly laughing; Char, my editor and friend, for your heartfelt dedication, wisdom, guidance, and hilarity; Dominick, an idea whiz and inspirational motivator; Erica, for saying yes and believing we can change the world. We are.

For all my anam caras, my soul friends, and guides on this journey: Darrell, Debra, Sus, Liz and Randy, Vivian, Jamie and Kevin K., June and John, Manny, Greg and Bonnie, Christine and John, Amanda and Michael, Nancy and Todd, Jaye and Tom, Roberta, Polly, Pat, Ron and Debra, Melissa, Tad and Caroline, Tara, Connie, Aveen, Dia, Jane, Ty, Scott, Steve, Kevin P., Brad, Hillary, Jan, Carla, Grace, and Christina.

For Beth, Dennis, and Maeve: for your deep love, creativity, and vision; Denise and Dai, you taught me how to hold deep pain, die to what was gone, and protect my happiness.

For my beautiful people: the Wood, Rollins, Conner, and Brinker families. I'm blessed to have you. You're always in my heart.

For all my committed clients: You have trusted my guidance and used these bravery concepts and techniques over the years, helping me refine them and make them true. Deep gratitude for your soul work.

For all my Lakewood tribe: Bev, Judy, Annie, Sylvia, Dana, Tim, Judee, Brian, Jackie and Jackie, Gaye, and everyone else I wish I could mention. I love you and am devoted to your loyal friendship for over four decades.

For my pillars in community: LinkedIn family, you are wonderful beings. Ashok, Michelle, Sejal, Andy, Michael, Martha, Melissa, Frank and Gretchen, I treasure your unceasing faith and support. Aquarians:

Mauricio, Bryan, Valerie, and Ana—we share archetypal vision.

For my recovery, spiritual, yoga, and meditation collectives: deep bows to all of you, and to my first teachers, Jack and Paulette.

For each one of you who have shown unconditional love, support, and companionship, and to my social media supporters: I appreciate you for who you are in your amazing uniqueness. You anchor me and give me hope.

Finally, for my husband, David, my soul love, who, with your bighearted creative style, has drawn 200 coffeepot love notes for me. You've unceasingly listened to questions and answered them at all times of the night or day. Your generosity holds me.

Introduction

It was after midnight, and my phone rang. My mind jumped and my heart raced; then suddenly it dropped. I thought, *no one calls me this time of night…at least not with good news.* I remembered the last time it happened. Each time the phone rings late at night I still tremble inside, *please don't let this be the call. I'm not ready. I'm not strong enough. No, not now…*I plead.

Are any of us ever really brave enough?

Fortunately, I already had some knowledge, but I didn't have the conscious awareness or the bravery training I needed. I didn't yet understand the full impact I could make on my two sons who struggled with addiction and mental health issues if I worked on myself instead of focusing my attention on helping them.

I'd been teaching clients about courage concepts and techniques for two decades. However, as I continued to face intense devastation and grief myself, dealing with my sons' problems, I realized I had to learn how to practice bravery so that it would kick in as an instinctive reflex under fire. I wanted to become fully equipped to be of better assistance to them.

That's what conscious bravery is; it's what I needed back then and still desire now: instincts that have become so well trained that courage emerges naturally. Since that call, I've received innumerable late-night or early-morning calls from my sons in crisis or in jail, from hospitals or treatment centers, emergency texts from their friends, or alarming door knocks from police or paramedics. Once, we were even awakened by first responders in our home, just outside our bedroom door when my youngest son called 911 on himself, afraid of what he might do.

Those dealing with loved ones with addiction and mental health issues more than likely have received, or will receive, those hard phone calls and unwanted visitors. Tapping into a deep well of bravery within and a repertoire of options and resources to choose from is essential in handling these times. This book, and my next book to follow, will enable you to ground in the truths and self-care methods, training you to tap into your innate capacity for bravery as you begin to put them into practice.

Rewiring and Transformation

If you love someone with addiction and/or mental health issues, you know that tragedies often arrive in more than threes; they just keep coming. But what is addiction? Addiction to alcohol or substances begins as a person's solution to their troubles. They perceive that their pain is unmanageable and long for authentic connection with others. Drugs or alcohol temporarily take the edge off. Substance use often progresses, morphing into the multiheaded beast of full-on addiction. This can turn our loved ones into people we may not recognize, who they don't even know themselves anymore. Addiction is complex. It's more than a compulsion or a craving; it's an inability to go without substances, alcohol, or behaviors, eventually leading to self-destruction. And this requires professional support. Relapses usually accompany addiction. There is no simple cure because the recovery process requires *rewiring*: with physical, mental, emotional, and spiritual sobriety, "a whole-soul makeover," accompanied by new routines, constant maintenance, and lifestyle changes.[1]

Going through the unimaginable, you may believe you cannot do what seems impossible. I've felt that way dozens of times and am here to offer you ways to pull yourself up, stand tall, and walk forward one shocked or exhausted step at a time, when so much around and within you seems uncontrollable. However, a primary way you can find some power and contribute to your loved one's whole-soul makeover is to create your own. Working on yourself first and being prepared for anything which might occur is required. This will give you the brave capacity to lovingly connect with them no matter their circumstances. Addiction is not your fault, and you can't control it, so learn to bring compassion to your feelings of guilt around their substance use.[2] A lot of the issues you face can be solved with your own personal growth. In this book, I invite you to develop the courage

---

1   Erica Spiegelman, Rewired (and The Rewired Workbook).

2   Alcoholics Anonymous.

needed to take brave, assertive steps with confidence, even when you feel depleted. Remember, lasting transformation begins with *you.*

Since you can develop self-control over yourself and your reactions, you are not powerless during the challenges your loved one faces. You cannot "fix" your daughter who grapples with unwanted addiction, or heal your depressed son. You can, however, become stronger, discover meaning, find clarity, rebalance, set boundaries, protect your happiness and live a life you love, regardless of what's presenting in the moment. And I know this is hard, but well worth it, as it's what I've had to learn and practice myself. You are not the sum of your overwhelm, or your unanticipated situation. You are a resilient being who can cultivate fierce and tender courage which will guide you and outlast these present circumstances. My friend, you are more than your fears and more than who you've been until now. You are a beautiful being who is in the process of becoming all you can be, with each present moment as your teacher.

The Wilderness of Addiction

Unknowns abound in the wilderness of addiction; yet you'll move through them by learning to adapt to change, embracing fear, becoming more comfortable with discomfort, befriending unpleasant feelings, savoring moments of joy, and beginning to rebuild the life you crave, free of whatever you feel is holding you back now. When things seem out of control it can feel overpowering. That's why you start consciously wherever you are to reclaim your own well-being and apprentice in the training of relentless courage.

If you're going through loss, confusion, or heartbreak because someone you care about is unwell or their lives are chaotic, disrupting your peace and happiness, you'll find the answers, tools, and methods to deal with all of it here. If what's happening to them is greatly affecting you, or someone you love is now gone or has passed away, I offer you my deepest empathy. Perhaps your loved one and you have incurred several tragedies at once. If so, you have my whole heart. We as human beings don't become braver just silently wishing for courage, though. Bravery will not magically appear with the wave of a wand. You need relief, inspiration, and techniques to handle whatever hardships have fallen in your lap. And it takes consistent practice to achieve homeostasis.

Both of my young adult sons have toiled through addictions, mental health battles, trauma, injuries, and huge legal issues for years. I've imperfectly managed the upheaval of other kinds of difficulties as well: divorce after twenty-one years, caring for my new husband through brain cancer, and then his passing, and deaths of my parents from Alzheimer's and dementia. I've collapsed in despair but have also bathed my way into self-soothing. Wrestling with adversity, I've used the self-care practices I modified for clients and have baby-stepped my way from fragility into tenacious bravery that sustains me. My source? Love. Unshakable love. I love my sons so much, I don't have the "luxury of despair." Cheryl Strayed coined that phrase, saying that she hopes we remember this the next time we break down. I do. I'm reminded of it when my sons fall and when I fail. My deep-down desire for bravery has become foundational in cultivating it consciously.

Your situation is unique to you, and you may face different issues than I have, but I've been close to where you are. We are in this together. In this wilderness, your unique journey is unparalleled, and the bravery you forge will be your own. The good news is that the seeds of bravery were planted inside you at birth. Everyone is born with sacred and innate valor, just as love is also woven into our DNA. This instinctual bravery is what you are now being called to develop. It's a privilege you are gifted. Your boldness is natural, yet it needs to be trained—fed with meaningful information and practices that strengthen it. Cultivating your courage via these pages will help you grow to be like a flexible, tall tree that can bend with circumstances but not break.

Terminology

There are many stages on the continuum of impairment from substance use, and not all use leads to addiction. Yet for purposes here, I'll refer to any sort of severe substance use or dependency as addiction. This book is about you, and what you need to do for yourself doesn't change whether your loved one is using substances, abusing them, substance dependent, "substance-use disordered," or addicted.[3] Additionally, for ease I am combining alcoholism and alcohol dependency together when I refer to addiction. This book is about how you can transform yourself and become braver while supporting your beloved. I won't use the word "codependency" because not all of you here are codependent. Many of you simply love someone with addiction and have a healthy desire to walk alongside them; you don't have a condition of extreme dependency upon your beloved but do want to communicate with authenticity, use strong boundaries, and do your own part to create healthier relationships without trying to change your beloved.

Practicing Bravery

What led me to write about bravery? A generally happy person, I have had a lifetime touched by grief. Many of us have. It wasn't until my late twenties as a new psychotherapist that I realized most of us only learn about bravery conceptually—there is not a body of specific courage protocols available to us. The unique mix of happiness combined with painful losses motivated me to understand how to foster this boldness through grief and still live with contentment.

I began refining and designing concepts, techniques, and practices, sharing them with my clients and using them myself. Ongoing education helped me form the techniques you'll find here. And over the course of more than three decades as a psychotherapist, I observed that what worked for my clients as I helped them find their way also worked for me. I've been in the trenches, learning as I go. Loving myself through my own trials, I've practiced these concepts diligently. A key, again, is to practice. I learned the hard way, because when I'd begin to slack off, I would start to feel more fearful or overwhelmed. So, I would begin once more.

I have lived awake, and I have lived unconsciously. Being present and

---

3   Jeannie Griffin, LMFT, LCDC: www.freshouttaplans.com.

awake is more painful but is absolutely more satisfying. Awake is the harder, the braver, and the more joy-filled choice. When I've hovered above the devastating times in life unconsciously, I've been angrier, discontented, made more mistakes and was without answers. There are many times when I was lost, couldn't access the needed resolve, landed hard, and failed. "I can do this; I will not indulge in despair" became a mantra during those devastating periods.

Authentic connections with my anam caras have been paramount. An "anam cara" is a Gaelic word I love for "soul friend."[4] Partnering with my soul friends and therapists, I've learned to open up in softness instead of parenting with hardcore management. Rather than offering unsolicited advice to my adult sons, or attempting to guide them, I try to listen, to interact, and to convey confidence in them; I tell and show them that we're all equal in going through these family challenges together. I will sometimes express how their actions have affected me—not to guilt them into change, but to be honest so they can face themselves and take accountability.

Genuinely relating to them with words and actions, I've learned to simply show that I believe they can become capable, independent young adults.

By spending time in quiet solitude and inquiry with my inner self, I keep walking forward more awake and present in my life. I've discovered that presence, here and now, is the only place of sanity and wisdom. I can't operate from the past or future. I protect my happiness, feeling the real pain of what happens without letting circumstances dominate my life. I smile often and metaphorically stand upon the ground of contentment. With whole-being awareness, not mere mindset shifts, I constantly rediscover what I can control when things seem insurmountably out of control.

Start Where You Are

These pages are a place where distress meets encouragement, with skills to manifest the heroic fiber you didn't realize you have. The fact that you're here means you're already braver than you know. Seeking assistance is

---

4 John O'Donohue, Anam Cara: A Book of Celtic Wisdom.

both strong and vulnerable. Start where you are. Just be yourself. Be real. Whatever you do impacts your loved ones. The development of your bravery will affect them through your love and actions.

Living with some sense of control and even flourishing is within reach. You can manifest courage by rebalancing, regaining perspective, and going forward even when discouraged. During tough times, tragedies often worsen then improve. Your intentions, wishes, and hopes are never enough and may leave you stranded in the fantasies of never-never land. There is no "perfect" courage, but by taking action you can become and remain braver. Learning methods to flow gracefully through repeated ups and downs is part of how you sort things out bravely.

I'm confident that you can hold your head higher as you devote your efforts toward renewal and your own unique and empowering bravery. I invite you to recapture your happiness, living from wonder and joy rather than despair. Let's walk together and begin.

BRAVERY KEY: LIVE FROM WONDER AND JOY RATHER THAN DESPAIR WITH CONSCIOUS BRAVERY.

CHAPTER 1

What is Conscious Bravery?

"There are two forms of courage in this world. One demands that we jump into action with our armor on. The other demands that we strip ourselves bare naked and surrender. Bravery is a curious thing."

— *Jeff Brown*

A devastating epidemic of drug and alcohol addiction and mental health crises surrounds us. We who care about or love someone with addiction can feel alone in the darkness, lost on an unwanted journey in a sometimes terrifying wilderness of pain and confusion, not knowing what to do or how to help.[5] I know this feeling all too well… it can seem impossible to even breathe. Yet when a loved one implodes, we are called to pick up the pieces and put ourselves back together for our own sake and theirs. We are pressed to cultivate the capacity to allow our pain and hold space for our own despair, while moving forward to carry on with unshakable bravery. When flying, we are instructed that should there be an emergency, if traveling with a child or someone who needs our assistance, we must put our oxygen mask on first before helping them with theirs, even when it's our own child. This can be a frightening thought. To be able to adequately assist a beloved amid crises, we are summoned to somehow rise above the circumstances, find conscious bravery, and help ourselves first.

What is conscious bravery, and how is it accessed?

Sandra Swenson, Tending Dandelions.

Conscious Bravery

Conscious bravery is the result of innate inner strength intentionally roused and engaged in action. It is not potential; it must be actively utilized. Consisting of a myriad of simple and practical elements, we initiate small acts of bravery daily without even thinking. It's this, in addition to fierce activation of strength and composure during turbulent times. Conscious bravery is a combination of being fully aware, combined with compassionate and daring behavior. It is courage that is alive and awake, partnered with unwavering love. Each of us carries it within ourselves day and night.

Yet courage that is conscious must be more than conceptual. It requires frequent practice and training, both during calmer moments and when in the murky trenches. The types of bravery we'll need to help ourselves and those we care about exist on a continuum, and with awareness, we can choose the style of courage needed. At times, we must become warriors, leaping into action. During other periods, what's called for is tender grace, our receptivity or surrender to the process of what this moment has delivered. Operating on a bravery continuum, over time we sharpen skills in consciously knowing what's necessary in any given moment. We learn discernment and develop confidence by imbedding brave words and deeds into our hearts, minds, bodies, and souls.

Just as we all have the ability to learn to swim, everyone is also able to train in developing the type of instinctive bravery which emerges when needed most. For example, in swimming, we learn not only different strokes, but also how to breathe, hold our breath underwater, or just float and tread water. We learn to dive from the water's edge and even leap off the high tower when we must act to save ourselves or someone we love. We are able to stand in stillness and quiet on the pool's border managing our discomfort, prepared for the cold water to come. This is conscious bravery. We learn how to control our breathing during danger and to flow amid adversity; to float during misfortune; to sprint when crisis calls for it; to lift our heads and view our surroundings when uncertain, and how to tread water when patience is needed. Sometimes the bravest thing is to do nothing and hold faith.

Getting unstuck and becoming brave is sticky business. It means taking measures with uncertain outcomes and no promise that the day will be saved. Conscious bravery is when you meet with resistance and make something new out of what was falling apart on a different day. You live in the now, not the past or future. Often your heart aches. Just as often, your heart breaks. Instinctive, relentless gutsiness is being able to proceed forward, doing what's tough or rough, even while feeling broken. This capacity comes from a space of compassion and tender empathy. You hone skills in loving because what bravery creates is sculpted from varied facets of love.

There is not just one right way to be consciously brave, not merely one particular type of bravery to utilize every time you need it. My moxie is not yours. It can appear in a hundred different ways on a hundred different days, in varying circumstances. This is because what you experience and what I—and others—may be facing are never exactly the same and require differing abilities in all sorts of alternative situations. You will know what is right for you when these challenges arrive.

Each new unique moment you encounter will require awareness and focus, altered perspective, insight, and varied bravery skills. This book will teach you conscious bravery concepts and techniques. I believe you will develop a newly felt strong sense of self-confidence as you begin to integrate these teachings individually.

There is only one you! You are the unique author of your own genuine daring and will cultivate it through repeated, informed, intentional choices to align with each presenting occurrence. You will birth and grow your personal expression of it, becoming capable for whatever arrives in your world with newly harnessed bravery.

What does it mean to harness your courage?

Harnessing Courage

The process of stepping into the waters of untested bravery can be a kind of beautiful ugliness. It's often a combination of doing something which is extremely difficult yet feeling empowered while doing it. You proceed from a choice among choices which may all seem insufficient. Yet with grace and strength you walk slowly forward, trembling on uneven ground that constantly shifts below. It's prickly and doesn't feel right, even when it is. There's fear, anxiety, and disharmony, knowing that sometimes what you are doing will create a sense of loss and pain for either yourself or someone you care about. You are able to convert the heaviness of sadness or disbelief into the small, brave, loving act you do anyway, one tiny step at a time. And you may walk limping, exhausted, short on faith, although with some form of hope. You dive head and heart first into that incredibly brave feat you are now able to undertake.

The audacious spunk required is multifold. There is the everyday kind, like filling out dozens of forms with your loved one who is applying for financial assistance for their multiple ambulance, inpatient, hospital, and various medical bills. Then there is the save-the-day type, when you drive for hours to the location of your beloved in the middle of the night because they unexpectedly called you asking for help after having been kicked out of a sober house with nowhere safe or drug free to go. Thankfully, various types of courage become more readily accessible because new insight and clarity arise from your innermost being, and you learn to harness it regularly.

Bravery that is aware springs from clear perspective and deep understanding, joined with love. Harnessing compassionate boldness, you are able to put the concepts learned into action. Awareness alone is never enough, because having and exhibiting courage means doing something to help yourself first, then someone else who needs your special form of bravery. Even if what you do involves patience, which I call "a not-doing that does," you are consciously engaged.

This kind of bravery activates through your awareness during alone time and in authentic collaboration. You're not meant to limit yourself to one or the other, either independence or teamwork. Braiding both together, you gain necessary skills while trusting your own distinct intuition and also making choices with enlightened collectives. Enlisting the help of tribes providing unity, comfort, understanding, love, and support is healthy. Combining these two together are both instrumental in spurring multifaceted strength.

Bravery can look like tenderness and sound like stillness. It isn't always tough as nails.

It can be messy, like rinsing out blood from sheets in the morning because your loved one got into a fight the night before, or tidy like boundaries you set for your self-care. This includes wisdom that emerges from within at the depths of your core. Informed awareness instructs you when to sit on something and do nothing and when to realize you cannot do this on your own and ask for help. Discernment grows over time and you're able to distinguish what's best, using sound judgment. Bravery then becomes a plethora of skills you are trained in and can access at any time.

Trust me, you'll need these skills in the wilderness of addiction.

The Courage to Lie

A fire crackled and blazed in the center of our huge teepee as twenty-five of us met ceremonially. On this warm June evening, we were seated cross-legged, tightly packed in a circular spiral. The dimly dancing firelight made the ritual more powerful while we marked my youngest son's graduation from a wilderness therapy program he'd been in for three months in the Colorado wild. He'd learned how to make his own shelter and sleep under the stars at night even amid the cold and sometimes fierce winds, and he'd become skilled at starting his own campfire from flint and steel. He and his peers and field counselors had walked miles together each day through the woods, meadows, and desert carrying heavy backpacks while opening their hearts, talking about their feelings, facing their fears, risking rejection but finding trust in each other. They meditated in nature, had fireside talks, did yoga at sunrise or by the full moon, sang in unison, made their own healthy meals, and uncovered their truth. Healing from pain, they all leaned into one another in supportive community. A band of explorers exploring mostly themselves, they were thirty miles from any town, alone out there. But they had each other.

I missed him terribly those three long months. Yet, a time of transformational healing had begun for him and our family. We'd handwritten letters back and forth to each other, sharing vulnerably and honestly. His dad and I were divorced but received our own family therapy along with doing intensive individual work while he was away. We had convinced ourselves we were ready for him to come back home.

Earlier that spring during his freshman year in high school and before wilderness, he'd already become addicted to alcohol and drugs as the solution to the anguish he sometimes felt inside, although we didn't know it at the time. The hunger to coat his anxiety and inner loneliness with substances was overwhelming for him. That's how it is with addiction; the alcohol and drugs seem like the *solution* to someone's pain, rather than a problem. Drugs are their primary answer, even if it's the wrong answer. People only begin lying, stealing, and sneaking out to get the substances their hijacked brains demand. For example, longing to belong, with only a driver's permit our son had snuck out in our car after midnight to meet friends and get high, then hit a pole and damaged the bumper. He lied to us about what happened, fearful about consequences. He'd done dozens of wrong things that weren't true to his nature as the beast of addiction led him astray, away from himself and from us. We couldn't enforce the boundaries we set. And neither positive nor negative consequences impacted our son. That's why our family therapist, educational consultant, and we parents all finally agreed that a wilderness therapy program was the best remedy at the time. There wasn't one right solution. I needed to make the best choice from the choices I had.

On the night of my son's wilderness graduation ceremony in the teepee, his seven wise peers, four field guides, and therapist were seated in a smaller circle directly around him taking turns while passing the talking stick, stating their "cares and concerns." Speaking of the beauty and truth seen in his character, they shared their confidence in what he could do in the near future, along with concerns about him and why. His dad and I sat close by, alongside our new spouses and our older son, touched and encouraged by what they were saying, raising our eyebrows and glancing at each other with amazement. In three months of living together day and night in the wilderness, these young men and their field guides had grown to know our son perhaps better than we did. Real and raw, they each said the same kinds of things differently: They loved his playful spirit and kind, caring heart, his hard work, and spiritual ideas. However, they also candidly told him they feared he would relapse upon returning to our homes. All the other young men in this group were choosing to go to aftercare programs or therapeutic boarding schools upon their graduations. They felt he needed more structure too. That would have meant a full year spent developing his new skills in self-understanding with clean, trustworthy friends and a stronger, professional support group. His inner "dragon," as he called it, required more time to be faced and tamed. They were literally afraid for him to find and rely on healthy alternatives for self-care while going to a public high school, instead of smoking weed and drinking. It was a final call to action. Their truth made us all choke up. But as his parents, we thought we knew better than his guides and peers. His dad and I were triathletes and, to our detriment as well as his, assumed confidently we could take on just about anything. Plus, our hearts were torn. We missed him tremendously and felt we had changed enough with improved parenting skills. Naturally, maybe even selfishly, we wanted to raise our son in our homes and believed we could do it. Our family agreed to try our own version of supportive "home aftercare"; if he relapsed, he'd go back to wilderness therapy again, then on to therapeutic boarding school for a year or more. We didn't realize he'd feel more like a failure if our plan didn't work.

Our son came back home the next day with us, but within three weeks at his high school he was expelled for getting drunk on school property. More than getting drunk, under the influence of alcohol he inadvertently got another girl so drunk she had to be taken to the hospital from the school. The dean somberly told me that a video camera showed him pouring alcohol from a covered bottle for the two of them in the library, and both were heard vomiting later in the bathroom. Because of the effects of alcohol and drugs, he was hurting someone else without meaning to, believing it was all fun. But I couldn't enable it. Empathetic for addiction's grip on him, I knew he had to be turning to alcohol as a solution to his inner pain and whatever torments he was attempting to alleviate by self-medicating. Yet knowing that through his misguided actions he had now begun walking a path of unintentionally impairing, even injuring, someone else tore me apart. I knew at that moment I could not allow it to continue and had to protect him from himself, while shielding anyone else with whom he associated. It was a gut-wrenching realization. I was the parent with the clear vision. I had to make this hard choice, on another even more life-changing occasion, when he was still under eighteen. Both times, I regret now that I waited too long, hoping for better outcomes. I wish I had been more aware, opened my eyes more to his suffering and his secrets.

In the room at the school with my son and the dean, I kept it together, listening to the news in quiet shock. But the next morning when I walked into my son's bedroom, I gasped; the whole room smelled so strongly of alcohol it was overwhelming. He'd been drinking so much that he barely staggered to his feet. It hit me that he felt like he'd failed himself and us. I felt angry with myself that I hadn't tuned into how hard that night might be for him. Why hadn't it occurred to me that he might continue drinking? With fear, sadness, and compassion, I said, "Honey, we're leaving to go get a breathalyzer test," and grabbed a huge water bottle and some food for him on the drive. At the test site, he was given a urinalysis too. His blood alcohol concentration (BAC) and THC results were shocking: he was high and drunk, and if he'd been driving and pulled over, he would have been given a DUI.

It was like being hit over the head with a brick. My knees collapsed beneath me, and I sat on the floor just sobbing. All at once, I knew what this meant, and a huge wave of sadness overtook me. We had a very serious problem here; my son was dealing with overwhelming pain and anxiety, cravings for alcohol and drugs, and impulses he couldn't control. The direction we were going wasn't working and we had to change it. He and our entire family needed highly trained, long-term professional help. And, I knew action had to be taken on short order to get him safely to wilderness therapy then on to a year of residential school in another state. My thoughts and heart told me that we would all have to give this everything we had *now*, while he was young, hoping to make a difference sooner than later. After a few minutes of conscious breathing and heightened awareness I was able to reset, facing this new now by surrendering to it rather than fighting or minimizing the reality of what had already occurred. Within hours, his dad and stepmom came to our home, we made calls and arrangements, and all four of us parents helped our son as he packed his things for the wilderness yet again. He convinced us he was willing and ready to go. But late in the afternoon, out of the blue he suddenly bolted up the stairs from his room and ran as fast as he could. He flew through our sliding back door, outside into the yard and was gone. We searched for him for hours to no avail. He had run away.

That night at 8:00 p.m., he called me in kindness from a landline to say he was okay and not to worry, then hung up. Our family banded together and located the motel where we thought he might be staying. Upon our arrival, the front office person confirmed a young man who fit the description of my son had paid with his bag of two-dollar coins, gifts I had given him over the course of his childhood. I knew then he was there. We parents walked the halls for hours, listening for his voice through every single door. Finally, two hours later, I heard my son speaking quietly inside one of the rooms. I talked with him through the door, lovingly urging him to come home, telling him that I loved him—we loved him. He wasn't in trouble, and we could figure things out. No answer. Total silence. I called him by my nickname for him: Sunshine. I begged and pleaded. No response. So we called the police, and a SWAT team of four men came. They spent an hour trying to get him to open that door but couldn't enter without permission. It was a harrowing night. I feared he'd leave the room and end up being another runaway we've all heard about who ends up dead but never found. I stayed in the motel until around 3:00 a.m., before deciding to go home and come back later that morning. My husband and I returned the next day, and my son was walking outside the motel. It must have been a rough night for him, too, so he agreed to return home on the condition that he didn't have to go back to wilderness therapy. He wasn't ready to be clean. So I lied—one of the hardest things I've ever done—and said okay. At that moment, I knew my bravery meant lying to him so we could ensure his safety. Taking care of him would require a trained team. He came home, and we spent quality time together in solitude, silently recouping from all that had happened.

On the hopes that we would find our son, we had already preprepared and arranged for a squad of two crisis interventionists to take him to wilderness safely. They were on call, ready to come to our home that night. My thoughts had been loud as I made this extremely difficult decision, but I did it by choosing to listen to my own truest self above all the noise.

When we'd settled in that evening and my son was in bed reading before sleep, with a burning rock in the pit of my stomach and what felt like sandpaper in my throat, I let two burly, professionally trained therapeutic crisis escorts into my home as planned. They talked him into going on the six-hour drive into wilderness therapy with them. When leaving his room, though, he tried to run again. It was a miserable scene, as the two men tackled my son, then restrained him. Finally, they talked him down, and he reluctantly got into their black Suburban. We all had gentle words, but the last thing my son said to me through the window as he shook his head was: "You lied to me! You tricked me! Thanks for sending me away, Mom." I felt horrible guilt, and tried to respond with love. "We're not sending you away; we're sending you somewhere to get help." They drove away, and I fell apart. I didn't want him to go. I said to myself: *We've betrayed him. Does he really have to go? Maybe this is the wrong decision. Why couldn't we do this? We have failed him.* My doubts and questions scrolled boldly across my mind like subtitles in a foreign film. Making this choice and sticking with it was the first hardest thing I've ever done. But I believe it positively altered our family's direction and may have saved his life.

What made me able to do this? Because I loved him more than I clung to my dream. He was my Sunshine. We were close. I wanted to have him near and be his loving mom, raising him myself, walking alongside him, comforting him on his journey. It took mustering all the bravery I had to let go of my dream and instead enlist professionals to give him what he needed elsewhere. Lying to him was unnatural and seemed so wrong, but it felt like a matter of life or death, so I forced myself to do it out of love. In all instances except for times like these, I abide by a policy of truth telling. I had to remind myself that I wanted him to have the chance for his young brain and body to develop without drugs and alcohol prevailing over his path or possibly killing him. I chose to believe in him and trust this process we were both a part of. I never gave up. I sustained the ability to handle my pain and was brave enough to surrender my previous expectations. The bottom line was, I finally realized he needed more than our family alone could provide. Among all of the hard choices, I knew it was the absolute right thing to do.

Even though he felt abandoned, I stayed present in my letters to him and lovingly engaged in our weekly family therapy calls with him. Honoring his anger and hurt with empathy, I didn't let it overcome me. But some days, I had to work tremendously hard just to get out of bed and put my feet on the floor in gratitude. I flew to see him every three weeks, and we'd hike and play ping pong together. We'd drink hot chocolate during conversations that were real and often difficult, but I showed him my unconditional love and confidence in him and us. In subsequent days and weeks, I moved through intense guilt, pain, sadness, and grief. Determined to grow my bravery, I breathed consciously, meditated with discomfort, cried my heart out, practiced gratitude that he was alive and that I had this opportunity to help him. I constantly reset and rebalanced when I could, did my own self-care diligently, and rediscovered my own unique version of contentment. I worked to guard my sparkle. Learned how to fill my own tank, over and over again, with lovingkindness. Starting small, I used the concepts in this book to know my true self, slowly and purposefully cultivating courage step by step. We had each other; we were in this together, and the main thing I could change in this mess was myself.

It was a hard year for him, and for all of us as we walked a flawed and rugged path. Yet with support in sobriety and kindness from his therapist and peer group, he slowly put his values back into place, began addressing inner pain and anxiety, and faced his inner dragon. His brain and body were free from drugs except for one serious relapse. He practiced self-love and self-care, got good grades, and learned a few things about friendship and loyalty. We parents each did our own individual work and family therapy and grew in awareness. We deepened our love, healed as we could, and learned boundary setting skills from a compassion point.

My youngest son has continued to have tremendous difficulty sustaining capacity to hold his pain in self-soothing. Though he's learning to face conflict, he battles a pattern of impulsively wanting to run from difficulties. I've subsequently had to become braver in expansive and more varied ways. Becoming more vulnerably strong has helped. I share this because I know that bravery for you will mean building on varying types of courage repeatedly over time. When we go through the fruitful darkness consciously, we can eventually lounge in the light.

You'll find your own way through the wilderness with bravery as your guide map.

Navigating the Wilderness of Addiction

You face such varied tragedies that all require a wide range of tools for fortitude to take on countless types of painful emotions, traumatic situations, and unexpected bumps along the way. The plans you make often change on a dime. When you have acquired an ingrained ability to choose wisely from your bravery toolkit, your metaphoric palette of paints, you can create what's best at the time for yourself while partnering with your loved one for healing by consciously constructing viable solutions.

It is so challenging to navigate through the harrowing wilderness of addiction while your beloved confronts their distress, hardships, and personal mental health. They live in an unpredictable world where they are relentlessly battered, physically and emotionally taken advantage of, losing health, self-respect, and hope. They and their friends encounter tragedy, sickness, loss of jobs, coming in and out of altered states, disappearing, and even dying from overdoses, accidents, and/or suicides.

You must develop conscious and extreme bravery to grieve these losses;

recover, protect your true happiness, reset, then maintain your own stasis under pressure, to become and stay authentic while tending your wounds and renewing your spirit. Be diligent. I have to; you can too. I know you can be brave enough to demonstrate care for your loved one or friend unconditionally without any expectation of a particular outcome. I urge you to work on being vulnerable and learn to handle your discomfort, holding space in kindness for your own pain. Please don't hold back your love in avoidance, or sever the relationship. Your unconditional love and unfailing presence will make all the difference.

Expert skills in courage are required to find your own way in the darkness so that you can link arms with your loved one and crawl or trudge together forward into the light.

We are pioneers in this wilderness and need concepts that guide us and truths to live by.

Pioneers

As parents and loved ones of these beautiful neurodiverse beings who never intended the difficulties they've incurred, we want to end misunderstandings, inauthenticity, and wavering boundaries by stepping boldly into our own truth. When insights emerge from practiced skills, we can begin to break free of generational patterns from the past, where our ancestors with mental health issues were viewed through glaring lenses, as if their addictions dubbed them such woeful terms as "inadequate," "sick," "psychotic," or "misfits." Our loved ones deserve our unyielding conscious understanding and support instead of harsh judgment and unfair shunning.

Bravery wakes us up as we pioneer into new and more honest perspectives of mental health and addiction with true empathy, love, and compassion. This expands with new research and information, allowing us to view our loved ones as the beautiful beings which they indeed are. We are becoming better equipped to acknowledge their neurodiversity and disease, no longer labeled as mentally ill. In other words, we see our beloveds as real, whole people with struggles, not as those whose issues and adversities define who they are. With evolving perspectives like these, we are gradually able to positively impact interventions and modify treatments received.

This is a much larger topic that won't be addressed in this book, except to note here that bravery in this arena of addiction and mental health means bringing new ideas to the courts and treatment systems that are still problematically wavering and, more often, broken. We can eventually halt or transform the drug and mental health epidemic because we will insightfully and courageously put our combined understanding into action and break stigmas. Together, we'll proactively impact outdated systems to grasp the fact that positive intervention and treatment for our beloveds works immensely better than cruel and archaic punishment modalities. Treatment programs need our informed input as they formulate creative and workable solutions for our beloveds and our families when "relapse" occurs.[6]

We and our loved ones have ridden the ups and downs of unwanted rollercoasters for months, years, or even lifetimes. Who wants to have a major mental health challenge or a life-threatening addiction fraught with relapses!? No one! Because all involved are on such a perilous ride, as their close-in parents and loved ones, it is easy for us to focus solely upon them. Conscious bravery teaches us we must continually practice self-care. We put down the zoom lens and pick up the mirror. Unlearning the codependency of enabling, managing, or trying to "save" our beloveds, we concentrate instead on handling our own rational worries and heartbreak, thereby granting ourselves the grace to extend genuine, loving, open arms of healthy caring.

Is it your desire to keep learning and be able to access this kind of awakened resolve and wisdom? You already have some of it now, and

---

6   There are so many researchers and writers whom I respect and are experts and advocates in the realm of addiction and mental health. Here are just a few whose work I recommend: David Sheff, Erica Spiegelman, Jeff Brown, Kevin McCauley, Brad Reedy, Sandra Swenson, Dan Siegel, Jeffrey Foote, David Hawkins, Bessel van der Kolk, Stephen Porges, Russell Brand, Gabor Mate, Melody Beattie, Allen Berger, Robert J. Meyers & Brenda L. Wolfe, Xavier Amador, Deb Dana, Rolf Gates, Janina Fischer, Pat Ogden, Alan Seale, Bryan Maynard, and Nedra Tawwab.

even more is accessible! Your courage will grow stronger by consciously developing it, practicing it so often that it's more than instinctual.

Keep reading.

You're becoming a bravery aficionado.

Bravery Aficionados

We are not weekend warriors; instead, we choose to develop into proficient and consistent bravery experts, training ourselves gradually into full-time warriors. Wondrously, human beings are born with the seeds of bravery. It resides in the core of our humanness. It's in our essence, along with the seedlings of every other universal gift, such as love, self-love, truth, beauty, creativity, loyalty, hard work, kindness, and more. All we need to do is develop them, practice, and use bravery alongside these other gifts in such varying circumstances that we begin to intuit what types of skills are needed when. Eventually, our courage is ingrained, and appropriate responses kick in instinctively. We become bravery aficionados. With harnessed courage, we no longer "Try to be brave; we are brave." We don't just want it; we live it. Adaptable and committed to contentment, we're not amateurs anymore. Bravery aficionados can assertively move toward what's difficult rather than run away from it. Less wavering, we consciously rebalance often. Our determined, graceful grit enables us to live with greater peace and serenity, finding ease in our days and nights.

If you're ready, hungry for this type of bravery, keep reading. Now you are ready to put it all together.

Putting it all Together

How do you graduate with the bravado that will answer every call and outlast your intensity or moods in varied situations? With ingrained emotional discipline and insight, you develop the necessary skills in operating on a continuous sequence of options. You are able to tap into your innate abilities for vulnerability and strength, grace and grit, tenderness and toughness. These are all flipsides of the same coin. You open yourself up and develop both with the ability to be vulnerable *and* strong. One solidifies and enhances the other, and you are more versatile with a wider range of options available.

Since mental fortitude is embedded in your sacred humanness, activating it is satisfying—sort of like expressing love. Framed this way, you allow yourself to exhibit your strengths completely and commit to developing them diligently. Partnering with both the known and unknown, you learn to lean into the power of change, able to manage discomfort. Just like when learning to swim you develop a variety of skills then put them all together, so it is with intrepidity. You meet your fears where they are and see them as advisers rather than adversaries. Savvy that you have little control over your circumstances, or other people's, you find the beginnings of resilience within yourself. Deep self-love is critical in the development of perseverance because it can be daunting to face your situation without it. Plowing on, you expand your heart-power to manage grief and catastrophe with backbone as you go—never giving up. You learn how to ask for help, and give it, through authentic connections. All imperfectly. People and things may still challenge you. Taking risks at times, you become more daring. Conscious bravery is cultivated as it is practiced daily then used under fire.

Your ability to see what's needed at any given time will improve, eventually becoming more precise and accessible. You'll begin to wake up with increased awareness more often, practice gratitude, maintain heightened attention, and be more present throughout the day. Doing so will protect your happiness and you'll be able to take on challenges as each minute unfolds, much differently than before. You'll find your own voice, hearing and following its many tones and variations, discovering your unique self over all the noise. It may be slow going and confusing at first. Just pace yourself; you can't tell your healing to "hurry up." Your current situation is one of the best places to learn how to develop ongoing courage.

There is no power without a softer, more empathetic touch. You imagine being that person you love. Walking in their shoes, living their life, you allow your heart to open. Informed by compassionate insight into their lifelong world and experience, you're inspired to be stronger than ever before.

Neither you nor your loved one chose this unwanted journey. I invite you to find your way through the wilderness by cultivating your own conscious, brave living. Do it for yourself. You'll become competent at staying solid, flowing with what *is*, or better yet, a bit of both. Setbacks don't have to be devastating. Living more awake, with vibrancy, you'll recover more quickly. Standing tall, you'll be like a rooted tree of graceful strength, a role model whose growth will impact the shared world with your beloved. You'll convey hope and emanate confidence in them.

Your path is here. Your path is everywhere you'll go this year, the next, and perhaps even the next. Don't wait for a more perfect time, my friend— There isn't one.

BRAVERY KEY: CONSCIOUS BRAVERY IS INSTINCTIVE, INTENTIONAL COURAGE IN ACTION.

Cultivate it and become a bravery aficionado.

In the next four chapters, you'll come to understand foundational bravery concepts. The first four essential pillars you'll need to build your courage are: befriending your feelings, becoming comfortable with discomfort, breathing consciously, and knowing that you are your essence.

Keep reading!

CHAPTER 2

Befriend Feelings: Allow Your Emotions

Rumi wrote this beautiful poem called "The Guest House." Each one of our feelings can be allowed, even invited.

The Guest House

This being human is a guest house, every morning a new arrival.
A joy, a depression, a meanness, some momentary awareness
Comes as an unexpected visitor.
Welcome and entertain them all! Even if they're a crowd of sorrows,
Who violently sweep your house empty of its furniture,
Still, treat each guest honorably.
He may be clearing you out for some new delight.
The dark thought, the shame, the malice, meet them at the door laughing,
And invite them in.
Be grateful for whoever comes, because each has been sent
As a guide from beyond.

I recently saw this: "Manifest Joy," which was crossed through with a big X. Written next to it was "Feel Real Emotions." It caught my attention and expresses what I call "Befriending Feelings." Allowing *all* emotions to be our friends, we don't avoid or exclude challenging feelings. To manifest joy within ourselves and in our lives, we cultivate the ability to feel all of our emotions, both the pleasurable or "positive" ones and the perceived negative ones.

Emotional Agility

It's brave to vulnerably befriend all of our emotions, to fully encourage and experience them without either filtering them out or dwelling upon them. To feel is real. When I've allowed each and every one of my true emotions to come as they are, even those that are unpleasant or seem dangerous, I end up having more joy.

Emotions don't always make sense. At times, our brains connect the dots from what's happening in the present moment to something that was stored in our minds as "similar" from years past, and we respond with bigger emotions than the fresh situation deserves. Sometimes we're triggered by memories or issues we haven't completely worked through. But it's not our feelings that we need to beware of; it's what we could do with them if they are not attended to and disallowed. If feelings are shut down, they take on a life of their own, becoming bigger, calling out for attention like screaming children. We can do odd and unhealthy things when our wayward, disregarded feelings take the reins. To respond with bravery and nonreactivity, we want to separate from our reactive thoughts and allow the oftentimes irrationality of our feelings. They can be beautifully raw, like abstract art. If we are able to view them as if we're in a gallery, observing and not judging, they are allowed to move through us more quickly.

Research shows that most emotions will dissipate in one to three minutes if they are allowed adequate space to move. They can whisk through us like gentle wind if we permit the breeze to flow unhindered. Additionally, we build emotional agility and resilience when we accept our unpleasant feelings with unconditional love—the same type of deep caring we feel for our loved ones.[7] We begin seeing emotions as part of us instead of intruders to avoid.

When we give our mind less power and operate with respect for our heart while permitting our discomfort, we can turn down the dial in our head. I love imagining the image of a dial or switch on the outside of my head and being able to turn it down as I bow with respect to my emotions. I'm not suggesting we live from a place of overemotionality. In fact, the opposite happens when we don't overvalue our mind, choosing instead to respect

---

7   See also Susan David's book Emotional Agility.

and listen to our heart. This is a balancing act. If we're able to practice this more in our daily lives, we are much less likely to bounce around frenetically, busy with compulsive actions such as obsessive problem-solving, overexercising, overeating, workaholism, or using substances to take things down a notch. Pacing ourselves, we bring our feelings along with us throughout our days. We calm the mess between our ears with our hands on our heart.

Old Programming

There is a powerful character on the television show Star Trek: The Next Generation, the version with the brilliant Jean-Luc Picard. This beautiful being is the complex *Data*. He's an android who morphed and became almost fully human. Why? How did a robot with an embedded chip as his commanding circuitry, a computer for a heart, become like us? Because he self-evolved to develop a huge heart. He began caring so deeply for others that he could wrestle with and even accept his fierce and genuine emotions. Desiring to be human more than anything, he overrode his bot programming. That's precisely what we as parents and loved ones of those with addictions and mental health issues must learn to do, amid seemingly insurmountable odds. We develop hearts that are bigger than our programs. In essence, we reprogram ourselves and our capacity to deal effectively with all of our conflicting emotions.

For years in my earlier life and before having children, I was never adept at identifying and understanding my feelings until days or even weeks after I felt them. However, in recent years, as I've developed the ability to outlast my fears and helpless feelings, I have embraced myself and loved much bigger than I imagined possible. I have been blessed with grace and garnered with the energy to go forward, even when in total exhaustion. Now I'm a bit like Data, intensely desiring to be genuine and authentic. I honor my feelings more than I want to stay stuck in old programming despite previous coding.

Inviting Feelings

We can feel many seemingly opposing things all at the same time. For example, when I heard the phone report from my oldest son's case manager recently about how well he'd been doing during his first weeks back in residential treatment, all at once I felt a combination of being joyful, surprised, happy, worried, yet slightly fearful of what might happen down the road.

It's important to notice, identify, and honor the complexity of such a potpourri, expanding on our capacity to also handle those mixed emotions in unison. When we are real and are operating from the awareness of our whole being—not just our thoughts—we're able to regard and contain our feelings in a sort of dissonant harmony. When we have loved ones who struggle with the extreme highs and lows of addiction and/or mental health, it is even more important to accept our feelings without a "story" or any judgment that's self-blaming, like, "I'm such an idiot; I should be over this." Without making ourselves bad, or anyone else wrong, we open our arms to innocent, pure emotion for a few minutes.

Giving concise descriptions of our feelings enhances our whole-being understanding of ourselves and improves our interactions with others because we're more clear and discard assumptions. Distinct words help us to claim personal agency. Emotions have importance, and by not neglecting what we feel, we can let them inform and advise our free choices. We live more purposefully when we expand our emotional repertoire like a wide array of colors on our palates. Like artists, we are better able to paint the lives we want to have with creative awareness.

Feeling our emotions dumps us in the gray area. We stop being so black and white, expanding beyond the five simple core emotions that children are taught: happy, sad, mad, scared, and disgusted. We *well round* ourselves, rotund with the capability to roll with any punches that circumstances bring into our worlds. I've been better able to handle the ups and downs of my sons and other loved ones when I color my world outside of predictable dotted lines, baring my soul with awareness of my truth instead of what I "should" or "shouldn't" be feeling. There is no "should" with emotions. We feel what we do, and that's that. Emotions have a path of their own, a fire that can either blaze or smolder. We're unwillingly drawn into the whirlwind of dramatic dust storms when we don't allow what *is* to arrive, in our circumstances or within us.

Additionally, by inviting all feelings without bias, we become better at not putting labels on or boxes around our circumstances, designating them as good or bad. Our young adult in recovery is just as equal to our friend's twenty-year-old studying at Harvard. Success is not defined by achievements, money, "things," or talents.

Magical Flexibility

I am not plagued by devastating emotions when I invite them in. But isn't inviting a form of tolerating, you might ask? Isn't normalizing a feeling like sadness, for example, a way of yielding to what we want to avoid? Or even encouraging more of it? Not at all. For example, when we grant our sadness, we thwart its exaggerated cousin misery. Misery is stored sadness inflated by ruminating thoughts over time. Misery rises like bread dough, as if we'd put sadness in a bowl and fed it yeast, fermented it, and grew it into something bigger than it originally was. Misery is sadness's tormentor. We can circumvent self-perpetuated torment by this process of befriending not just sadness, but all of our emotions.

When we allow ourselves these feelings of helplessness, fury, shame, or fear with compassion, the unpleasant sensations pass after a short time. Then when we're ready, we are able to consciously release them. Albeit, it may take some work to get there. Being more kind to ourselves, we freely invite whatever comes into our world with greater ease. Able to find our balance and stay more steady, we're not knocked off our feet falling prey to circumstances or feeling tossed into oblivion. We're endowed with a form of magical flexibility.

An Emotional Repertoire

Knowing what we feel is easier if we can practice being aware of what's happening and identify our emotions. Let's try it together right now. Think of a difficulty you're having currently. Notice the emotion, for example:

"I'm agitated, and my stomach is upset." Additionally, identify the feeling: "I'm scared" or "I'm sad." Next, *be with* that feeling. Empathize with yourself: acknowledging, "This really hurts." Now you can truly *allow* it with compassion: "Ugh, this feels overwhelming." *Accepting* the emotion behind your feelings may be really hard. Stick with it. Slow down, instead of rushing in to fix it. *Honor* it. Really *listen* to its message: "I hear you." And take a moment to express it—sigh, cry, growl, journal, draw, speak it aloud, or even scream. Collapse on the couch if you need to. Now, observe what has changed. You're likely altered in this new moment. You're becoming more familiar with yourself and your process. Do you believe you can handle it? If so, let it go. Release it as much as you can. Later, set some time aside for self-care to recenter and rebalance.

Just as a pianist knows all the notes on the keyboard and the myriad of ways to play them, familiarity with all of our emotions is similar. Include all feelings in your collection. Even shame, guilt, or a sense of hatred have an important place in our emotional repertoire. When we judge emotions, we're segregating them with unfair bias, by playing only the keys that comprise the major, or happier-sounding keys. Get to know and play those deep, low notes too. Become adept at playing the minor chords. There's an important time and place for soulfully sad, darker, poignant music.

Bring tenderness into your experience and notice sensations without judgment, without attaching a "story" to them. I try to think of myself as a friend who is kind to my more unpopular emotions. I sometimes imagine the feelings I like least embodying a human form sitting right next to me. I empathetically ask them, "What's going on?" and give them my unconditional presence and soothing ear.

Try this: In kindness, be with your hurt, sitting next to it. Offer yourself empathy and comfort. Tend to your feelings as you would a wound, giving them your attention, without any expectations. You may feel helpless, or without a sense of knowing, as if you don't understand what you're doing. Allow the sadness and discomfort of that. Simultaneously try to forgive yourself for any mistakes you've made or things you weren't aware of while experiencing your feelings. You may notice regret, self-doubt, not trusting your intuition, or the frustration of "not knowing any better," some or all of which may have brought you to this place. Breathe love and compassion into your being and from your inner self; inhale with self-compassion and exhale with lovingkindness. Genuine tenderness is a healer of other emotions.

I do this myself often. I sit tenderly with my hurts, offering comfort. Here's a window into why.

A Mother's Love

I'm barreling down the highway toward Denver, trying not to speed and charged with adrenaline. Butterflies are going from my stomach up to my head. It's 10:00 a.m. on a Saturday in early spring. Driving the sixty miles from my hometown to the Mile High City with almost three million people, I'm hoping to find my oldest son. I'd made this same drive yesterday. The Front Range mountains to my west are a blur as I'm thinking about what happened two weeks ago, how he has been homeless on the streets since then—out of contact, with no phone, no money, and no identification.

Two weeks prior, he had called me from jail saying he'd been arrested for trespassing. He had already detoxed while incarcerated and told me he was ready to go to treatment. Defeated and ashamed, he opened up about wanting his mind to heal from various drugs he had craved then given into. He'd had trouble with psychosis for months but was very clearheaded as we spoke then. I felt immense relief, and our connection was loving. He vulnerably pled for me to bail him out and take him directly to the long-term healing center we'd been in contact with before this relapse. He told me he'd lost his ID's and felt he had lost everything except for his desire to stay clean. After talking with him about his sincerity and commitment, I agreed to pay his bond at the jail and pick him up at 7:30 in the morning two days later. I trusted him. Anytime he had requested treatment in the past, he'd always followed through. He told me he was very grateful, and we exchanged loving goodbyes. I felt deep empathy for him and tender compassion. I arrived at 7:30 as promised, and waited, but somehow he got past me and left the jail, hitting the streets with nothing but the clothes he had on. He'd simply disappeared. I'd been anxious about him for two weeks since, with no word from him. I filed a missing person's report, but to no avail.

Just yesterday afternoon, he finally phoned me. He said a few cryptic words; his voice sounded anxious and confused, dropping in sadness, then he hung up. I knew he'd called to let me know he was alive. But I thought more about what he said, something about the security administration, and realized he was asking for help. I sensed that he felt like a failure again and didn't feel loved. I called the number back immediately, and the phone was answered by a homeless day-shelter staff person near the capitol in Denver. Relieved, at least I knew where he was! Feeling hopeful, I jumped in my car as fast as I could and raced to the shelter, but he was already gone. I spent the evening searching four nearby homeless shelters, remembering his voice and how he seemed to be calling for my help. But all I saw were weathered and sullen survivalists, our quiet and weary homeless friends, and none were my son.

I was up early the next day, sick to my stomach thinking about how, knowing him, he had likely been awake for days without sleep. I was motivated to find my son, though. As I felt my emotions rising, I honored them yet did not allow them to overtake me. I had to keep my composure. I refused to give up. I didn't want him to finally crash or overdose with no one noticing and end up dead on some back alley without being found for days. I wanted desperately to see him gain, to look him in the eyes with love and offer to take him for a meal and a shower in a hotel if he wanted one. I didn't want him to feel any pressure from me, just love. Back in my car, I sped to Denver. Nearing the capitol, I suddenly had a knowing that I would see him. I felt reassured and certain, yet still nervous—all at once. My intuition told me I should watch along the sidewalks. As I slowed down, I began to search, right and left. Driving this way for miles, I felt that he was close. Rolling down Broadway, I suddenly saw what looked like him. I thought, *Is that him?* He was so thin and was limping. Excited, I said out loud: "Yes, it's him!" He looked unhinged. My heart pounded hard within my chest, aware that it's not only his body, heart, and soul that are injured, it's his mind too. He was filthy. Well, he hadn't showered for two weeks. I pulled over quickly, double-parked and put my flashers on. I bounded out of my car; he was half a block away walking toward me, talking aloud to himself. I called out, "Hi honey!" Speaking more gently now, bursting with a smile and tears in my eyes as we walked toward each other, I tenderly uttered "I love you."

He was costumed like some kind of warrior-magician, dressed all in black with a red sash tied around his head and red bands encircling his right bicep and knee, holding up a makeshift wand. I felt overjoyed to see him. We looked straight into each other's eyes, speechless. Time stopped and there was nothing else but that very moment. I stared deeply into his eyes with tenderness, but he wasn't there. Something else had taken over, casting a spell, casting me away. To my disbelief and heartbreak, he turned to go the opposite direction. But even as he began to run, I was sure of this: he knew my love.

Why did he run? He was altered, on drugs. His brain had been hijacked by addiction. The monster of addiction was dictating, overriding his need for food, safety, water, even love; he wasn't rational. There is another dark and hostile realm, and he was glancing out at me through it. But in that world, he had a glimpse of deep truth: I was there with him, and he was loved. He could feel it. I know.

Addiction is a beast. It takes over those we care about and tries to overcome their souls. The feelings and truth of love can rise up and win, though. Emotions are powerful, and love is the fiercest force. That day, I honored my feelings, and that day, my son knew he was not alone.

I had so many intense emotions during that time, and after. Befriending all my feelings brought me consolation. Over the following two weeks a slow miracle occurred, and the happy ending to this story happened when he called me again. I picked him up and took him to treatment with a fresh start.

Chances are, if you're reading this you already know the extent of a parent's love. We never give up. Love has so many feelings mixed up in it. It's the solid unifier, collecting the strength of our compassion and the tenderness of unconditional kindness, holding our fears in the mix. Love is like glue, a collaborator, and it holds all of our emotions together.

Collaboration

When we really listen to our feelings as if they are our friends, they become slightly less intense, less overwhelming, and more manageable. They have a voice, and they simply want to be heard. Pause. Give a listen to what your feelings have to say. Thoughts don't have a heart; emotions do.

One crucial reason to make friends with our emotions and become familiar with them is so that when the biggest devastations occur, we're well prepared and are able to handle the accompanying huge emotional blasts we feel without lingering in states of dramatic ups or downs. Those crises will come. Everyone will experience extreme challenges and suffering in life. Let's practice on easier days and be ready for anything!

When we don't stuff our true feelings, avoid them, deny, or minimize them, we are less reactive, less compulsive, and less guarded. We don't build up resentment or avoid things through substances. We are less defensive, have fewer outbursts, and are more grounded. We're more fun to be around, and we have more fun. Laughing easily from our hearts and souls, we can tap into joy. Becoming comfortable with all of our emotions allows us not only to manage drastic trials, but also to move more smoothly through them and to live a life we can enjoy. It's a delightful benefit of befriending our feelings.

I'll gladly sit in a room full of people who can be real with their feelings, support each other, and talk about what's meaningful with them any day. Resilient, genuine folks with strong, tender hearts are the people I laugh hardest with and for whom I will show up anytime, day or night. They're there for me as well.

Just as when we accept the rainy weather outside, it doesn't start pouring harder; so with our feelings. Inviting them simply means that we go beyond tolerating them. We collaborate with them and can move forward having learned lessons from what their messages bring us. We're more awake and aware in the moment and can then live from greater presence, more comfortable with the discomfort of the now. Happiness becomes more readily available to us.

BRAVERY KEY: BEFRIENDING FEELINGS IS POWERFUL MEDICINE FOR TRANSFORMATION INTO HAPPINESS AND EVEN JOY.

In the next chapter, "Become Comfortable with Discomfort," we'll see how the application of befriending all of our feelings gives us the ability to handle even the most disagreeable, harsh, or gut-wrenching combination of emotions and experiences.

CHAPTER 3

Become Comfortable with Discomfort:
Partner with Change

"Generally speaking, we regard discomfort in any form as bad news. But for...people who have a certain hunger to know what is true—feelings like disappointment, embarrassment, irritation, resentment, anger, jealousy, and fear, instead of being bad news, are actually very clear moments that teach us where it is that we're holding back. They teach us to perk up and lean in when we feel we'd rather collapse and back away. They're like messengers that show us, with terrifying clarity, exactly where we're stuck."

—Pema Chodron

Unexpected Visitors

Imagine that you hear a sudden loud knocking, an unexpected pounding like a rhythmic drumbeat, and it prickles up the hairs on your neck and arms. Then—silence. You quickly walk to your front door and peek through the small window to the porch of your home. Four acquaintances are there and resume hammering with their knuckles repeatedly: Change, Fear, the Unknown, and Devastation. They're large and ominous. You freeze, as dread sets in. Hoping they'll go away, you may not even open the door, might hide in another room, or escape through a window. But they have arrived! Somehow, they barrel in uninvited, are inappropriately noisy, then stop and stare you down. What do you do?

When confronted with such demanding predators, instincts immediately tell us to freeze or run. However, by pausing in the moment and breathing consciously, we can be still, listen intently, observe quietly, and decide what to do in a few minutes. Staying with our discomfort and moving through it into appropriate action differs from befriending our feelings because extreme discomfort is a *complex combination of the most challenging emotions*—shock, dismay, fear, disappointment, anger, shame, and even hatred. Managing this acute distress requires every ounce of energy and wisdom we've got since the culmination of emotions in discomfort overtakes us like a tsunami. We are immobilized unless we take the steps to *self-soothe* with solace, *hold space* with strength, and assertively *surrender* to what *is*.

Even a few minutes of self-empathy and yielding to the moment must occur before gaining clarity and figuring things out. First, we bring *solace* to ourselves in our situation. Compassionate comfort is a powerful, driving force. It is the soul's way of taking over temporarily, and affirming: *I can do this*. Second, we stand in our strength while *surrendering* to what *is*, without cowering. This robust stance is a valiant choice with active realization that we can't control or undo what has happened. By seeing things as they are, rather than downplaying or resisting them, we can wisely take the next courageous step required. Instead of being passive or reactive, we're more consciously and purposefully involved in *whatever is*. Temporarily waving the white flag, we partner with what's happening, unable to do anything that helps our loved ones in this moment except soothe them—and ourselves— but this process will help us to be braver and more clear minded in our overall responses later.

Shattered

It was a chilly evening in March a few years ago when discomfort once again knocked on my door. My oldest son and I had shared a nice morning earlier together, connecting over coffee. But I came home at dusk and saw two moving silhouettes through our back window. I opened the door and the energy in the house felt frantic. Two people were sitting on our living room sofa, and I didn't know one of them. My son was leaning in to the other person. I felt shocked, anxious, and sad all at once, and this memory is etched in my mind; it encompasses all that ensued for months after. Sometimes we remember a food we like but now find distasteful because the last time we ate it we became ill. It's that way for me here—I remember that morning as the last pleasant time my son was not in treatment, injured, homeless, unwell, in jail, or psychotic for a year.

I walked toward them with trepidation. Body memory reminded me that both of my sons had been the leaders of dozens of eclectic teams of displaced drug users, and I felt wary. A wave of sick apprehension ran through my stomach. My son was trying to soothe her crying and shaking. I felt shaky too. I wanted to comfort her, but I was scared, and remembered to state my own needs clearly. Feeling guilty, I firmly said to him: "Remember our agreement: No one I don't know is allowed in our home, and no one brings chaos into it." But my son was in an altered state from the previously clear and calm condition he'd been in that morning. He talked at lightning speed, and in between his usual English he spoke a language that was otherworldly, not making sense. This only happened when he was on a stimulant, like Adderall, cocaine, or methamphetamines. Even though I felt tremendously uncomfortable, I exhaled deeply and anchored my feet on the ground.

My son told me she'd been threatened at a party, wanted a ride to the bus station and a ticket to get out of town, but neither of them had money. He asked me for help. In the shape he was in, I knew he shouldn't be driving. After seven years of addiction highs and lows, I knew enough to trust my intuition that this was not likely the full story, and there were shady characters hiding in the shadows of greater truth. I wanted to exert a strong yet loving boundary, but I was overtaken by severe discomfort, even anguish, in my whole body; my thoughts raced, heart pounded, throat tightened, and stomach churned. My job was to protect my son and myself, not someone I didn't know. I told her, "You need to leave our house, please. The bus station is within walking distance." Maybe not the best thing to say, but that's what came out of my mouth. Looking at my son, I added, "How about you stay, and we have a calm night?" He became angrily distraught and got up, obviously deciding to take her without my blessing. I doubted they were going to the bus station and felt a sense of doom, fearing that things were going to get bad. When I went outside, it was too late. They were gone.

It wasn't until the next morning that I saw my son again. I knocked on his door. He moaned. Entering, there was dried blood everywhere—on his face, hand, and all over the sheets. Seeing him wounded and covered in blood was harrowing. He was suffering, and I hadn't been able to protect him from this injury, from his pain, from anything. It was a mom's worst nightmare. The aftereffects of addiction chaos and a mental health escalation left me shattered, powerless, unable to help him. I knew that he had to be as battered internally as he was physically. I said, "Sweetheart, are you okay?" He awakened slowly, "Hi, Mom." I asked him again if he was okay, looking around the room for any signs. He said, "I need to go to treatment." There was a long pause. Sitting up, he said, "Police brought me here. I was arrested and charged with a DUI earlier, but because of the pandemic they didn't put me in jail. Can we go get my car; then can you take me to treatment?" Feeling relief that he wanted help, I said "Sure." As extreme discomfort overwhelmed me, I felt intense fear, shock, pain, panic, even anger at his situation. I couldn't stand the torture of this anguish. So I breathed consciously, did my best not to judge my feelings, and stayed with my discomfort in self-soothing. Allowing myself to feel into the agony, I surrendered into this new moment. Soon after, I felt a sense of solace. Thinking more clearly, along with my body feeling lighter, I knew I could take the next brave steps.

I listened internally to my whole being, even though something needed to happen quickly. He required expeditious help. I had a full day of patients scheduled, was reluctant to cancel, but my son needed to receive immediate medical care while getting clean with the support of detox. For about a half hour while he was showering, then as we made breakfast, I listened to him as he told me where he wanted to go for the integrative, supportive care he needed. The entire time, I breathed consciously, gave myself and him soothing, grounded in presence, and reflected. That's what allowed me to do what I knew I *had* to do. I helped him pack, and three hours later he was in an Uber to the best detox and treatment center on his insurance, which *he* had chosen. It was not a center that offered the mental health care I felt he needed, but staying with my discomfort helped me remember how important his own agency was in the process. After all, he could receive psychological treatment soon enough, once he'd received first aid, therapeutic detox, and had been clean for a month.

This story is about you too. In brave decisions, you sometimes have to make the best choice among choices that might not necessarily be the best at the time. During the most alarming periods in your life, you must find *solace and surrender* to what *is* for a few minutes or hours amid the chaos. Change, Fear, the Unknown, and Devastation arrive unexpectedly when you love someone who has breakdowns and experiences altered states. In the Broadway musical *Hamilton*, Lin-Manuel Miranda sings, "In the eye of a hurricane there is quiet." This is exactly what happens when you allow it: In the middle of the whirlwind, you discover a way out. Leaning into discomfort, you can find the eye to see.

There's not usually only one right choice; there may be many possibilities, so you comfort yourself through storms then do the best thing soon after. You need ingrained dexterity with techniques that work to discern. Becoming comfortable with discomfort takes maximum effort but is a powerful learned skill, an even more complex and involved capacity for bravery than getting to know and honoring feelings. It is the vehicle you use to stay in the eye of the storm, unbearable though it may seem, eventually emerging to stand on solid ground later. It's all too easy to leap from the apprehension of distress into taking immediate action. But that can be unwise and lead to further reactivity or even more trouble. You must develop emotional, physical, and mental intelligence, the capacity to get out of your racing mind and pause first before proceeding.

Oftentimes, it is just plain difficult to stop your ruminating mind. You divert fears by pushing them aside, distract yourself, or simply reframe a way of looking at things with false positivity. Willing thoughts to pass too soon only brings them back with a vengeance when your guard is down, such as in conversation with a safe loved one, or in the middle of the night when least expected. You may toss in bed, have a nightmarish dream, or wake up alerted as they return for attention. However, listening to your gut-wrenching thoughts and paying close attention to your feelings is a validating and empathetic step into bravery.

Self-Soothing, Holding Space and Surrender

You did not cause your loved one's behavioral health hurdles or instigate their substance abuse, and you cannot cure them. Fraught with discombobulation at times, how then do you remember to bring these essentials together amid hardships? *Habit* embeds your capacity. Recall what we practiced in *befriending feelings?* You committed to allowing your emotions to be valued. By permitting your thoughts as well, you hold space for your discomfort and mental pain.

In this way, you experience kindness and soothing during the most tumultuous moments, showing up and training your bravery into being. The magic that roots your courage comes from combining *self-soothing, holding space, and surrendering* not only to the moment but also to the process.

Try a slightly different exercise now, focusing on an experience you've had of agonizing discomfort. In kindness toward yourself, and to develop new strength, recall and allow those feelings and thoughts instead of battling them. Tapping fully into what you remember, what's happening in your body now? Does your neck feel tight? Maybe your tummy hurts? Are you biting your lip or averting your eyes? Draw your attention to subtle details. What are you thinking? Fears of your loved one's failure, injury, or death? Do you have looping repeats of self-degradation as you beat yourself up? Has your soul dropped, making you question God or your fate? Bring in the soothing power of compassion to handle your discomfort in this harrowing situation. Consciously breathing into your pain, tenderly go inside and lovingly offer yourself the deepest, soulful hug you would give your best friend. Holding space for the acute unpleasantness will move you in the direction toward being able to surrender to what *is*. Notice the shift; and in this new moment, pay attention to whatever you're thinking as well. Reframe your perspective if needed. It is profoundly intimate to link arms with your discomfort and will enable you to be stronger and move forward.

Familiarity with Discomfort

I know how hard this approach can be, requiring repeated recommitment and focus upon the prizes of greater contentment and solid courage. I dislike the sensation of helplessness more than any other feeling. I've often felt powerless due to the adversities and trauma both my sons have been through, and that inability to help them has often been affirmed by additional chaos or tragedy which ensued. Yet when I specify my helplessness, I no longer feel avoidant or weak. I know what's happening, and I'm right there with it. Holding space for powerlessness while soothing it with tremendous empathy makes me more vulnerable and stronger.

To get acquainted with tormenting intruders like Change, Fear, the Unknown, and Devastation, become familiar with what it's like to be you. In your own unique process, which emotions are highly excruciating for you? Being familiar with what makes you most uncomfortable will help you recognize it and prepare for when that feeling arrives, training you in the emotional endurance you'll need. You'll be able to say to yourself: "Oh, here's that feeling I hate. I know how to handle it."

Our capacity to fully be with and engage our discomfort can become an automatic response, providing us bravery to partner with the forces of Change, Fear, the Unknown, and Devastation. The beast of addiction feels like it nails us and our loved ones at times. Mental health eruptions can shatter our worlds. But we are not stuck, not nailed down, not overtaken. We can rediscover serenity after turmoil.

BRAVERY KEY: HOLDING THE AGONY OF OUR DISCOMFORT WITH DEEP SELF-SOOTHING CREATES A METAPHORIC MAP TO THE CALM SPOT IN THE EYE OF A HURRICANE.

In the next chapter, I'll speak in a variety of ways about another foundational concept in managing discomfort and pain: breathing consciously.

CHAPTER 4

Conscious Breathing: Bring Steadiness into Crisis

*"If our breathing is chaotic, our minds and emotions will
be chaotic as well. If our breathing is steady, our minds
and emotions will be steady."*

—*Rolf Gates*

When faced with a crisis and things seem out of control, we often panic.
The first solid thing we can do to steady ourselves is bring focus to our
breathing. Taking a conscious breath on a moment's notice instantly
relieves pressure as we find some ground to stand on.

Conscious breathing is not just "deep breathing" or "centering"
ourselves. Although those are superb practices for finding peace, breathing
consciously is an even more powerful method to achieve greater stability
during any critical moment. What can we turn to when our hearts
are broken or when we're under fire? Our dependable go-to is inhaling
and exhaling with awareness; bringing in self-empathy adds a sense of
support. Stuck in our heads, we often forget that our very capable bodies
are already working to calm us down. By tuning into our lungs and heart
space with kindness, we "wake up" and fully arrive in any painfully harsh
moment, with our hearts and bodies partnering to alleviate the panic. This
specialized type of breathing is an unwavering resource available to us at
any time, in any place.

When people tell us to "take some deep breaths" during a crisis, they're
forgetting the magical ingredients: empathy and awareness. For precise,
optimal execution of any kind, deep breaths help, but merely breathing

during an emergency isn't enough. We need to breathe through our whole being with empathy and awareness.

Self-Empathy and Consciousness

What is self-empathy? It is powerful kindness directed toward ourselves for what we are experiencing. Harnessed with this compassionate force, we're more ready to decide how to respond with courage. Without being armed with empathy while breathing under duress, we usually aren't fully conscious. And without full consciousness in our circumstances, we can't truly act with bravery. We can only enact the courage we need when aware and equipped, because bravery is not a reaction; it's a purposeful response.

What is consciousness in the context of breathing? Synonymous with awareness, consciousness means both broadening our perspective—viewing the situation as a whole from all points of view—while also narrowing it to see ourselves and our needs in it as well. People often react instead of responding during crises because of frantic thinking about what needs to be done soon, instead of being fully present with what *is* right now. As breathing consciously becomes natural during responses, we stop fighting circumstances and steady our ground. Thus, breathing with alertness is the doorway into the realm of active choices.

Life is hard enough. On top of typical daily challenges which most people face, those of us who love someone with life-disrupting mental health breakdowns and addictions have added ongoing hurdles because of the calamities that often arrive. We need every bit of comfort and relief we can get. To move away from dominating, often fearful thoughts amid a chaotic moment, we can connect to our automatic inhales and exhales with focus and lovingkindness. Becoming more aware and clearer in perspective, we can soon proceed into the next brave step while maintaining broad awareness. Breathing with consciousness through discomfort helps return our steadiness when we "can't think straight" under threat.

Breathing Deliberately

When a sudden emergency throws you off balance, your anatomy changes; body and mind go into hyperalert. To manage the crisis, you need answers. Yet to find workable solutions, you must first calm the panic to feel safe. Conscious breathing helps you *work with your body* to counteract its instinctually alert response.

By breathing deliberately, your whole being comes into awareness of what's going on inside you and details about the moment at hand. Current research shows that what's occurring in the body is just as important as the circumstances, so paying attention to that helps you respond best.[8] Emotions are directly impacted by our breathing patterns.[9] Keen concentration on both the breath and compassion for pain caused by your situation is what transforms conscious breathing into the gift of the abundantly rich medicine needed. You will find steadiness through this direct vehicle into your body and heart, which are preferable places to reside for a few minutes when thoughts are racing or full of fear by offering the golden warmth of self-empathy. Absorbing the tenderness within you, feeling near-immediate relief, you can wobble back up after being knocked down. The rhythmic breath rocks you back into balance. Once you have reestablished a sense of safety, feeling less under threat, you can discover the best solutions with what's available in the moment.[10]

Conscious breathing also gives your body the flexibility it needs to respond appropriately during disruptive moments. The soothing breath can either slow you down or speed you up, ground you or elevate you. For example, if you're panicked or on alert, specific styles of deep, deliberate breathing help you to steady yourself by activating the parasympathetic nervous system, which oversees the slowing of your heart rate. If you are undermotivated, other types of breathing like hyperventilating spark the sympathetic nervous system which accelerates your heart rate, elevating your mood and reducing stress. The primary mechanism that creates all of your experience is the body. You actively participate in improving your

8   Janina Fisher, Transforming the Living Legacy of Trauma (2021).

9   Emma Seppaia, "Breathing: The Little Known Secret to Peace of Mind" (April 2013).

10   Deb Dana, Polyvagal Exercises for Safety and Connection (2020).

relationship with it by breathing consciously. Awareness helps you know which type of breath is needed. The goal is to utilize breathing to feel steadier, gain clarity, then make the best decision of how to do whatever is necessary given the situation at hand. You need ingrained methods of adaptability to handle the challenges and trauma which addiction and mental instability present. Consistent, conscious breathing makes you adaptable.[11]

Calm Parents and Loved Ones

Several months ago, one of my young adult sons phoned me at 8:00 a.m. on a Sunday morning saying he had fallen asleep at a stoplight and was with four police officers. He said they were calm and nice and were trying to talk him into going to detox. He agreed to go and asked me to come and get him. Speaking quickly, he sounded very off. I said "Sure," and my husband and I arrived at the busy eight-lane intersection fifteen minutes later. My son had shaved his head that morning, and we found him sitting in his car wearing a long, bright red robe. He got out slowly to greet us. I walked with him around his car and over to mine. And I breathed, very consciously. I felt scared, shocked, and anxious, but my breath brought me peace and strength, enabling me to stay real, openly raw yet capable. Repeatedly that morning, deliberate, empathetic breathing helped me immensely as we drove to two detox centers, with long interviews and drug tests at both. It took several hours, but my son was finally placed.

Many events followed, yet an overwhelming sense of gratitude engulfed me. He hadn't been injured, had miraculously not hurt anyone else, and was now in supportive treatment. I attribute much of the composure I felt to vigilant breathing. Since he picked up on my calm breaths, my son was also more steady and at ease, able to do the next brave thing for himself—detoxing in a locked unit for three days.

When we as parents or loved ones are tranquil in these types of situations, our energies influence those dear to us and they feel safer, more relaxed

---

11   Peter Levine, Healing Trauma (2005, 2008).

themselves. Serene breaths help regulate them since humans are designed to reset with safety cues coming from others.[12] To help activate or calm loved ones down, we must have that capability ourselves.[13] We can show them the way when we know how to uncomplicate things. Actively exhibiting grace and strength through the breath gives us greater control. How do we remember to breathe consciously amid pain, a setback, or under threat?

Commit and Practice

Committing to practice conscious breathing when calm makes it more natural during difficulties. Motivation to *not* being undone by your heartbreak, panic, fear, terror, or devastation will remind you to use the breath to arrive in that space. Just like a soldier, you learn by doing, and train when not under attack. Promise yourself that you'll practice it morning and night, aware of how it empowers your courage. You'll be reinforced by the relief you feel from breathing purposefully. The more you do it, the more you'll want to! Consider putting a reminder into your phone so you're not just committed, it's scheduled into your day.

Try with me now for just three minutes to practice, so you're more ready for disruptions that will come. Pretend you've just heard some very tough news and you'll need to make a hard decision within an hour. You stop first, and take conscious, soothing breaths.

Keeping your eyes open but looking downward, be here in this moment. Be aware of your breathing and how you feel in your heart and body. Don't judge; just notice. You may have thoughts about the future or the past. Continue to focus on your breath. Breathing in, your nostrils and lungs are filling; breathing out, you feel release and space. Inhaling, you are right here, with self-empathy. Exhaling, you are alert. Your body is strong and

---

12   Stephen Porges, "The Anatomy of Calm," Psychology Today (October 2021), regarding dysregulation and coregulation by those around us.

13   Daniel J. Siegel, Pocket Guide to Interpersonal Neurobiology (2012), The Developing Mind, and The Whole-Brain Child, on attachment, integration in empathic connections and healthy relationships.

here to assist you. Bring softness to your heavy heart, and take pressure off your burdened mind. Stay attentive to the wavelike rhythm of the breath, tapping into kindness with pure self-love coming from your essence or soul. Saturate yourself with the strength of empathy from deep within. In this present moment you are experiencing support. Your whole being is here for you now, saying: "It's ok. I'm right here." Breathing in and out, aware, fill your bubble of presence with compassionate understanding. Your presence and body are holding you. You're regaining your footing. Now, stop and notice: What did you experience while breathing in this more-aware way? What's different? Take note; the value will remind you to breathe consciously again and again.

Breath Techniques

There are a myriad of breath techniques designed for different purposes. Choose one or more styles you like, using them as a basis while you bring in the awareness and empathy pieces to make them fully conscious.[14] Schedule breathing into your day with a reminder on your phone or planner: 7:00 a.m., breathe deliberately for one minute; 8:00 p.m., breathe consciously for two minutes. You won't make it happen without believing it's essential to your health and is necessary!

Ujjayi breathing is one of my favorites. By creating an ocean-like sound in the throat, it promotes life-force energy. It has jokingly been called the Darth Vader breath (which helps to do it), and many people find it especially activating for strength and bravery. Another prompt is to take three deliberate breaths during any transition: when leaving home, getting in or out of your car, walking through a doorway, or taking a bathroom break. Add awareness and empathy to your breath, and it becomes conscious! Sighs work wonders too. Sighs are useful blessings when you feel uncertain yet must persevere through unanticipated times. Via a simple sigh, you can land fully in your body and in the moment, releasing stress. Anchoring,

---

14   A few breathing techniques I recommend are: pranayama (yogic breathing, with varieties like ujjayi breath, lion's breath, or alternate-nostril breathing), star breathing, box breathing, counting breaths, pursed-lip breathing, Wim Hof method, holotropic breathwork, and Somatic Respiratory Integration (SRI).

you return to presence where you will take the next step. Any position anywhere is the realm for intentional breathing.

The Doorway

Breathing consciously is the doorway into almost everything we want: greater calm in our bodies, relief from doubt, clearer thinking, managing fear, rediscovering faith, clarity, real and raw bravery, and access to optimism. When it's ingrained, we can extend its benefits to our loved ones with greater ease. This magical breath is the archetypal arch into the current moment. Thankfully, breathing with awareness and empathy is free and available to us whenever we need it. Sparked by conscious breathing's positive effects, we feel more awake and brave, better prepared for whatever comes next.

BRAVERY KEY: BREATHING CONSCIOUSLY IS AN EMPOWERING FORCE. WHEN WE BREATHE THROUGH A CRISIS, WE ACTIVATE BRAVERY.

Conscious breathing is also a ticket into our essence, the subject of the next chapter.

CHAPTER 5

You are Your Essence:
Discover and Manifest Who You Are

"Begin to look for that piece of you that led you here to yourself... If you have yet to come to know this part of you, if you've never come to really know this gentle heart within your center, open your palms out in front of you, facing toward the sky, and reach out to meet your essence. Let it fill your palms and spill into you. Let it source for a moment with love and honor and gratitude."
—Sarah Blondin

Socrates said, "Know thyself." When it comes down to it and someone asks who you are, do you know how to answer?

Many people are far away from knowing who they are. They either try to push it away because they don't feel safe with others knowing, busy themselves to stay distracted, or act like someone they think they should be, not true to who they actually are. It takes a lot of energy to put on a charade trying to be someone we think we *should* be, especially during the toughest times.

Hundreds of my clients who are parents and beloveds of those with psychological issues tend to focus on how their substance-dependent young adult *children or partners are doing.* They've told me they don't have any idea who they are outside of their situations, roles, qualities, accomplishments, or talents, so they don't know how to unleash their inner bravery. Most of us overidentify with one or two aspects of how we present to the world, defining who we are via what we *do*, how we *look*, or what we're *dealing with*. We limit our perceptions of ourselves to either our minds, emotions, bodies, skills, roles, talents, jobs, or circumstances as we describe who we are. Yet these are merely outward expressions of us, not who we really are inside ourselves. This chapter is about discovering our genuine selves and manifesting more of who we want to *be* so that we can activate our courage both every day and under fire.

Who You Are

Your essence is who you really are, as the deepest, most sacred and authentic part of yourself. It is the inner wellspring of pure love. Everything you are and know is anchored in your essence. It's your source for all that is good: bravery, soothing, companionship, wisdom, truth, kindness, power, faith, beauty, and grace—all universal qualities. Directly connecting you with the Divine, nature, all sentient beings and the entire universe, your essence makes you human and vibrates with your beingness. After all, you are a human being, not a human doing.[15]

As Carl Sagan famously said, "We're made of star stuff." Your essence is also then your golden nature, your shining brightness and your warmth.[16] You are born gloriously radiating from your inner being. Each and every one of us is. Imagine your essence as a hub of connectivity. The golden energy strands of your essence interweave all of your various selves together: your qualities, parts, and roles. In addition, it joins your whole being: body, mind, heart, spirit, and the vital energy surrounding you in presence. In other words, while you are not defined by your body, mind, heart, intuition, and energy, your gilded essence expresses itself through all of these.

Your essence is the seeing, observing aspect of you. The source inside of you for calm and focus, it is your direct link to the wisdom that already

---

15   This phrase has been attributed to both Kurt Vonnegut and Wayne Dyer.

16   Darrell Grant's beautiful song "Shine" is inspiring.

resides within. Some call it your Inner Being,[17] the Seer,[18] the Observer,[19] or the Knower since it is the human *being* part of you that views without judgment, observes without fear, and knows without any false story or projection into the past or future. In some traditions it is called your soul. I prefer the elegant word "essence."

As the origin of your life force that makes everything work, when your body and/or mind isn't functioning or up to par, your essence guides you back into better health and greater equilibrium. It unites all your other primary parts, keeping you alive: your heart, lungs, and brain. It is who you have been since birth or before and who you will always be throughout your life until death and beyond.

Put simply, your essence is your inner home. Being interwoven with your essence, you are never alone, and you are always home. You can go inside to your powerfully safe haven without fail. Connecting to it can become the most satisfying form of soothing because it's always loving and supporting you. Your essence is unwaveringly available while others may not be consistently accessible. If someone else makes you feel better, that's icing on the cake, but it can't be what sustains you. You must practice and learn to access and rely on your own inner essence, rather than depending primarily on others for love and support, or to nourish your well-being.

Who You Aren't

You are not your thoughts[20]; they are just ways to receive, sort, and store information. Thoughts inform you, help you process data and recall things, but they pass. Your mind and perspective changes. You're not your emotions either; feelings are important, yet they are simply how you experience and process what happens. You're not even your body. It is a temporary

---

17   Eckhart Tolle, The Power of Now.

18   Michael Singer, The Untethered Soul.

19   Jiddu Krishnamurti, The Observer and the Observed.

20   Steven Covey, "We are not even our thoughts," The Seven Habits of Highly Effective People.

container for your whole being which will change throughout your life; you will become sick at times, might get injured, and will ultimately pass on. Your cherished talents and skills are gifts which have been cultivated, yet those don't describe who you are. Your honorable roles as a parent, wife, son, or sibling still don't encompass your beingness. Circumstances are situational and stuck in time. They are culminations of events occurring in your life or world at this moment but won't last and don't define you. You are not your fears or your paradigms; you're not your worries, your sadnesses, your highs or lows. You're not what you give or lose, nor are you the result of any of your accomplishments or failures. Although you're not your dreams, they are from your essence allowing you to manifest them into reality and make them come true. Your job is valuable and may even be your calling, but you are not limited to these designations which may change repeatedly over time. Who you are is not what you do in any way; those are your actions. You are so much more than the culmination of any outward expression.

Get to Know Yourself

It is vital to discover who you really are, and it's crucial for increasing your capacity to become adaptable and resilient. If you don't know who you are, how can you become braver, gain insight into your issues, and move through the adversities your loved ones and you face? Just as you become closer to your friends through quality connection, by spending time with who you are, you'll get to know yourself better and can even become your own best friend for life.

If you can dig down and become familiar with your truest self, that's a tool to get you through hard times, and you'll carry out what you need versus what other people want you to do or be. When you know who you are, it's easier to identify an expectation that isn't coming from yourself. Knowing your essence strengthens your bravery and lends to the ability to shake off what someone else thinks or expects of you. Connecting with the genuine you in deep compassion is healing, and you feel better through being your authentic self.

Understanding who you are means listening to your inner voice, even if that means straining to hear it. Knowing your essence and what you want is a foundation for developing bravery. Since you may be plowing through the unrelenting hardships which addiction and/or unsound mental health bring, you need solid anchoring and optimism. You also need to set boundaries. Rooting from within, hearing your own voice and establishing your limits comes from your essence because you *are* your essence.

As a parent or loved one of those with psychological issues who may also self-medicate with alcohol and drugs, you might often seek out advice from clinicians, treatment programs, lawyers, or friends. You can get lost in the maze of counsel, not clear about what to do. Unless you know your truest self, it's all too easy to do what someone else thinks you should do. It's overwhelming trying to move through devastating trauma unless you know who you are and what you need. With your wise, loving best friend inside you, you're clearer, stronger, and able to be bravely discerning. You'll weigh advice, then do what's best for you and your loved one.

You are Unbreakable

Intentionally become very familiar with the vibrant hub of who you are so you're able to access and call upon your unbreakable nature at a moment's notice. Familiarity is the precursor to knowing *intuitively* how to respond appropriately and bravely—leap into action or do nothing, or some variation in between.

If your family or beloved is in the wilderness of devastation, you may feel alone, too, and need a solid place to go, a refuge for soothing, direction, and answers. Your robust essence is that sanctuary where you can revive, return to contentment, and rekindle bravery. Crises at hand cannot destroy you, and your essence reminds you that you are unbreakable.

The Miracle of Your Essence

Let's face it, sometimes you need miracles. They don't always arrive. Yet you still have the knowing of something greater within you, the miracle of your essence, the direct line to the infinite and the Divine. Partnering with your essence, you can feel a guiding peace even through the most seemingly disastrous hardships. When confusing and traumatic events occur, consolation comes from your essence because it's linked to the dynamic power that controls the universe. Suffering can be overwhelming, and things don't always make sense. Tragic events like death and suicide occur. Understanding that you won't always understand everything, being in touch with your essence reminds and encourages you that somehow you will get through this.

Strength pours forth in unexpected ways when you operate from your essence. How? You abide in vibrant self-love so thoroughly that you have more tenacity along with compassion for yourself and others.[21] Perhaps most importantly, you can find and cultivate your bravery in the darkest depths. Your essence renews hope and provides purpose. Staying connected to it with unwavering trust in something greater, you trek forward out of grief and helplessness. One foot in front of the other.

You need to know your essence intimately and learn to *be* it as it is your lifeline, generating ideas which pull you out of despair. It is inspiration's magical fuel—producing the kinds of soulful creations that nurture and move you out of a narrower viewpoint. Open up to creativity: draw, journal, play an instrument, write a poem, or sing, and you will find that imagination provides renewed perspective. Lighten up by listening to music, paying attention to notes and lyrics with greater meaning. Go outside and play in nature or visit a friend and joke around. Powerful association to the surrounding world is enhanced by discovering your genuine self.

Spend Time with Your Essence

Seek out your sacred essence by simply breathing consciously and going inward—the bond already exists! Focus on the place within you that feels like it is this safe hub. Visualize your loving essence, and for a few seconds breathe into it, exhale from it, and hold an image of its vibrancy. You can do this during reflection, in a quiet moment, while moving, any

---

21   Dan Siegel, Mindsight. "Interoception" is a practice of becoming aware of different parts of our bodies, and I teach it to connect to our essence.

time, any place.[22] Tend to your essence by becoming fully aware of its presence as often as you can. Try opening your arms fully as you dial into your truest self, then hold yourself in a loving embrace. There's an invisible power source inside. There you are! The fullest nature of who you are and permanent home are with you right now. There's only one you, one unique individual you. Knowing who you are is intimately for only you to uncover. Perhaps you long for others to depict you, but you are privileged to decide that yourself.

Your essence may feel unfamiliar to you at first, but don't let that deter you from doing the inner work and spending time there—regularly. Make a concerted effort to get to know *you*. As E. E. Cummings said, "It takes courage to grow up and become who you really are." An aspect of bravery is seeing and being your true self, overriding cultural or familial influences.

Over time, you'll come to enjoy being with your indispensable essence. More familiar with this hub, the golden threads connecting it to all parts of you will begin to engender not just peace, but also gratitude and joy. Manifesting the happiness you want to feel will increase motivation to continue going back to your essence frequently. Don't depend on changed circumstances to make you feel better. Your beloved may have ongoing relapses or need psychiatric care. What will evoke relief is finding solace within, as your essence becomes the primary source of respite. You can smile, laugh, and feel moments of bliss more often when not defined by your situation.

Connected to the Universe

Years ago, I felt like I was inept as a parent, comparing myself with others whose children didn't have life-disrupting struggles. What made me unhappy was longing for particular outcomes with my sons. Both of them have been homeless (not because I wouldn't let them live in my house) and in jail for months at a time. Those circumstances were terribly

---

22   My friend Bryan Maynard has said, "Our experience of our own 'Being' is love experiencing itself."

heartbreaking. When I was able to live from my essence, I found some relief; I remembered that neither they nor I are defined by our situations or psychological health. Whether or not they're clean or mentally stable, we're all still whole and connected to the infinite through our inner beings.

Being aware of this link to our mysterious universe has helped me put circumstances in perspective. Trusting the universe, I could trust what is divinely connected to my essence. I've been able to live with faith regardless of my sons' choices, states of being, or where they were living. Our children need our strength to see that they can get through adversity too. If we're falling apart, how can they muster the faith needed on their own? When my sons were homeless due to drug-induced altered realities, I found comfort knowing that they always had their inner home.

It is encouraging news that you can never lose who you are. Even in death, your essence lives on. If your loved one faces tsunami-like hardships, you both have this inner well that always provides strength. If you feel lost, in your essence you are found—never lost, never alone. If they seem lost, trusting their essence will guide them on some level.

One with others and with the Divine you are uniquely interconnected. You are a radiant being, luminous in your existence and your expansion. Seek to understand and know who you are, spending time with and relying upon the vibrant love and gratitude coming from your own best friend for life. Solid and unbreakable, with awareness of your essence, conscious bravery will emerge from this soulful home.

BRAVERY KEY: RELY ON YOUR ESSENCE AND YOU'LL KNOW WHO YOU ARE. YOUR BEING WILL EMERGE, AND BRAVERY WILL MANIFEST OVER TIME.

Since our essence is the hub of our whole being, we are ready now to dive into what whole-being awareness is in the next chapter.

CHAPTER 6

Whole-being Awareness: Beyond Mindfulness

"When you expand your awareness, your energy flows freely. You're more flexible, balanced, and creative. You view yourself and the world with more compassion and understanding. You have more energy and are open to new possibilities."

—Deepak Chopra

Summon the idea of "mindfulness." What does it mean to be mindful? Becoming more attentive and awake, not just going through the motions. Conscious while doing something, whether it's really tasting food when eating, experiencing awareness while writing an email, or being fully present when talking with someone. And even though being "mindful" is a superb practice for "paying attention on purpose to present-moment phenomenon without judgment," "mindfulness" as both a word and a concept is limited.[23] The concept has been a great stepping-stone in the field of awareness but is not the end-all. Our minds are already too full!

Oddly enough, the mind is often the very source of human troubles, perpetuating inner suffering and actually preventing the fullness of awareness sought! The mind alone isn't capable of activating the presence desired. The word "mindfulness" automatically identifies with the mind by conjuring up the image of the mind as the only source of being in fullness. This is not true, nor what the aim is here. The goal is full-bodied,

---

23   Traumatology with Dr. Nicholas Barr, Ologies podcast, May 27, 2019.

wholehearted, soulful presence, along with conscious connection to experiences and other people. What were thought to be mindful responses were actually created by whole-being awareness.[24] Consciousness is required for both well-being and bravery. Yet, it's not focus from the mind that is the source of awakening into the present moment.

In addition to mindfulness, the word "heart-mindedness" is also often used to convey what is actually much more than wisdom from simply those two realms: heart and mind. It is the whole being that evokes a breadth of compassionate experience. During difficult situations, the whole being leads the way out of unproductive emotional reactivity into proactive responses. Instead of merely "listening to the heart," we listen to the whole being. Thus, it's not awareness coming solely from the heart that springboards awakening either.

Six Zones of Experience

Whole-being awareness is tapping into your world and experiencing it from six zones: *heart, body, mind, essence, intuition,* and the *energy* around you, showing when to take action and when to be still.[25] If there's confusion or agitation within you, that's a crucial time to pause, restore presence, and gain your bearings. Aware of your whole being and listening to data from its six regions, you are able to gradually transform and build greater satisfaction into your life no matter the circumstances. The magic of heightened, sensory awareness happens when the whole being is engaged, allowing then for bold steps to be taken into the unknown.

The wake-up call into consciousness needed for bravery comes with complete awareness from all six realms in unison, not just the mind, or even the heart; it's obtained by the entirety of wisdom available to humans

---

24   Alan Seale also uses the phrase "Whole-Being Awareness" in his book *Transformational Presence*, yet his definition of it is much different, referring to it as "the intuitive mind and heart intelligence."

25   Our energy field is a sixth zone of awareness, because our energy, or chi, is an extension of our whole being. Recent research suggests that who we are doesn't end with our skin—it surrounds us—and we are interconnected with others and with the quantum field. See Dr. Dan Siegel, "Mind, Self and Consciousness" (2020).

in any one moment. Instead of "I *think*, therefore I am" (Descartes), it is: I *am*, therefore, I am.

Whole-beingness provides not merely a source of knowledge, insight, and wisdom, it accesses the power needed in any moment to step into the heart, the mind, the essence, intuition, and energy, or whichever realm is needed most for what bravery is requiring. This is especially crucial to override the complex confusion that often accompanies challenges faced by family members and those we care about who are suffering from substance abuse or mental health, and helps in rebalancing. When overwhelmed by the fog of helplessness, pain, or terror, tapping in with total awareness you are able to experience a sense of safety and containment, then stand on solid ground and proceed with courage. Moreover, this six-level sensory awareness capacity provides the gift and the grace to make the environment and the whole being interesting places to live.

Sometimes from being wholly aware, a specific domain may call out for attention. For example, a courageous realization may occur spontaneously in the *mind* to alter perspective. By accessing and engaging the *heart* realm, one may finally be able to access and manage extreme discomfort or have the ability to speak up about a tough feeling like shame or fear. New recognition may happen in the *body* as well. It may summon attention via a stomachache that, without a vibrant awareness, might otherwise be pushed aside as a minor occurrence. With consciousness, an *intuitive* alert is acknowledged as a sense of trepidation which can then be acted upon. Each zone might beckon for consideration or response in varying situations.

Adaptable

Your essence and your complete consciousness are direct links to the energy inside and around you. Energy is a creative force which sparks inspiration, resourcefulness, and adaptability. Any time you tap in and notice, you'll likely feel an energy shift within you even if it's slight: when waking up, brushing your teeth and hair, showering, eating, reading emails, working out, hearing podcasts and news, listening to friends, talking with family, and smiling at strangers. Being aware of these energies, you'll feel more awake and able to experience enhanced vitality. Everything is impacted within and around you when you are tapped in. When you live moment to moment in a present, full way, you're more flexible and creative. There is a boldness to being whole, living energetically and instinctually with breadth. You can easily access the clearer mind and loving heart you need to move into braver actions with awareness of energy, assessing any given situation then doing what's best. Of course, this takes time, along with consistent, diligent practice. When you're fully present, you're spatially aware of everything going on, not just the stimuli that disrupt you, such as the actual situation or the rumination of your mind that magnifies it. You're adaptable.

Able to embrace any situation, you attend to things in the moment, taking on your challenges with a combination of tender self-empathy along with strength. Being present, you move more easily into joy, too, not holding back with dread that experiencing some joy might mean you could eventually lose it. Knowing that everything comes and goes, and each minute is different, you are less impacted by fear and live with greater contentment. You're receptive to possibilities. Suffering and happiness can abide compatibly together in your bubble of flexible presence.

With whole-being awareness, you have the ability to be emotionally agile. Living awakened in your everyday life, you tap into your pain more easily, without fear that things will be overwhelming. You can also laugh in a moment of joy because you're not fixed upon staying overwhelmed!

The Benefits of Whole-being Awareness

Do you sometimes feel like there's a mess between your ears? If so, you are not alone. Human beings often fixate on unproductive thoughts. Your brain tells you there's a good reason to worry, stay fixed in the past, or live from fear. When you live more instinctually from total awareness instead of from your mind, you can alter your former perceptions. Able to wisely rewind from the future back into the present moment, or fast-forward from the past into the now, you awaken into what is actually here because you know you are more than your thoughts. In the thick of what's happening to you, you know who you are.

Being fully aware, you'll receive informative wisdom from your entire being, which can literally and figuratively save you and those you love from unwariness and resulting predicaments. If you need to respond immediately to protect your beloved from danger or an overdose, when you're consciously tapped in you may choose intuitively to do it. Yet if it's more beneficial to hold back from something, like not running after your beloved's friend who just stole pain pills from your medicine cabinet, being wholly aware will inform you.

Additionally, an all-encompassing awareness helps you be more courageous and make important choices when faced with the unwanted, the unexpected, or the unknown. When you "see things as they are, (you) can take action in a wise and discerning manner."[26] If you're feeling anxious, with a churning stomach, tight shoulders, and a racing mind, frenetic energy may surround you. Challenging or traumatic news about your loved one will immediately spark worry or panic, and your distress is not merely emotional; it shows up as mental anguish, physical symptoms, soulful despair, and/or chaotic energy. Yet when you become aware of all that's going on in the six realms of your being, you can use data from one part to help you manage another. For example, if you haven't heard from your daughter for three days and your intuition is telling you that she is in danger, and your stomach feels queasy, too, you may think about it, then listen to your heart as well. Tapped into all realms, you might decide to text her roommate to check in on her. This happened to me once, and it saved one of my sons from an overdose. With mere mindfulness, you might discount your thoughts and tell yourself erroneously, "It's none of my business; she's probably fine, and I'm overreacting." As Mary Oliver puts it, "There is nothing more pathetic than caution when headlong might save a life, even, possibly, your own."[27]

---

26   Dr. Dan Siegel, "The Healthy Mind Platter," May 2020.

27   Mary Oliver, "Moments" from *Felicity*.

A Whole-being Scan

Most of you reading this book have experienced shock, confusion, loss, and grief from mental health or addiction issues causing fears and even terror that numbed or traumatized you. All of these wounds are part of what lead you to reengage, heal, seek wholeness, and to wake back up. Total awareness delivers you into clarity and steadiness. Wisdom from your whole being tells you that it's possible to attain greater health, restoration, and even contentment. Checking in with your six zones through a whole-being scan, you can know this with comforting certainty.

It's simple to take a minute and become fully aware by doing a quick scan of all your zones. With some conscious breaths, tap in. Ask:

1. What is happening inside your heart, emotionally?

2. In your body, what are you experiencing, seeing or hearing?

3. What are you thinking?

4. What is the deepest part of you, your essence, saying?

5. What are you intuiting now?

6. What do you notice about the energy around you?

That's it. See what happens for you, putting all that information together. Go a little bit further now and reflect upon an experience you had when you were upset in the last few days and register what was happening in these six areas: your heart, your body, your mind, your essence, your intuition, and the energy surrounding you. Over time, conscious awareness can become like riding a bike or swimming for you. All of it will rapidly come together the more you practice and learn to appreciate the valuable data you take in.[28]

What you acquire from your scan and why you're doing it may vary.

---

28   I first learned the "4 Lines Check" at Open Sky Wilderness Therapy and expanded it into my own version of the Whole-being Scan.

Sometimes you'll pay more attention to your essence, for soothing or to remember a guiding truth. Other times it will be more important to notice your body's wisdom: that the hairs are prickling on the back of your neck and you're feeling anger or fear but didn't know it. On a different occasion, by doing a whole-being scan you may note that the energy surrounding you is highly charged, and you want to bring it down with calming compassion. Another time, you may prefer to attend to your surroundings, noticing what you're seeing and hearing without judgment. This can come in handy when you're faced with tough new information, and you want to take it in without reacting then develop a response. Each of your realms has its own intelligence, and by purposefully listening you'll gain deeper and broader clarity than ever before. You'll learn to put it all together in a moment of vibrant awareness through your entire being and will feel the benefits on many levels with this type of being awake. When you need to give one area more attention you'll know it, because it will call out with a louder voice.

Yearning and Practice

What will help you allow yourself to yearn for bravery? Desiring courage activates the belief that it is not just a hope but a requirement for all you go through. Committing to it is then easier and follows more naturally. Don't hold back: Let yourself really crave bravery. You want added peace and desire the ability to be more daring. These are both companions of this vibrant awareness. As you cultivate greater harmony throughout your entire being, you will discover the gates into bravery open from accessing data about all of you. But don't get discouraged if you have ups and downs; they happen repeatedly as you learn all the strategies that build your courage.

The Path to Your Bravery isn't Linear

For me, it began nine years ago, the week our candid family coach gave it to me straight. She said something like this: "Your sons have severe addictions. They also have ADHD. They will be embarking on a long trek of recovery, and that usually means relapses because bumps and big falls are part of this challenge. You've got to do your own work, and be ready. You're part of a family system, and the only person you can change is you.

Their recovery may be up and down for years. Or decades. Or longer. If you begin to use the tools you've got under your belt, you can help yourself and help them. Even if they don't change, you'll alter your family system."

Wow. This hit me hard. Yet it motivated me. I knew there was no predictable timeline or how their own unique recoveries would look. Back then, all I knew to do was use techniques to work on myself, but I was slow in the applications and at times couldn't see that managing or trying to save them was getting in their way. I thought I was being helpful.

Committed to changing my part in our system, I returned to doing scans more frequently. Through an awakened state, I could usually notice when I wanted a sense of control. By paying attention to my whole self, I would hear my heart ache when I was afraid or notice my looping thoughts search for control when I wanted to respond as a manager, rescuer or enabler. More conscious, I could nip it in the bud and work on myself instead, calming fears and regaining sovereignty over *me*, the one person I *could* change.

I knew that ADHD is a mental health issue all its own, that people who have it are fraught with impulsivity, longings to feel better, or have social skill issues which make them feel bad about themselves. All these challenges can lead an impetuous person with the seeds of addiction in their DNA to crave a substance for escape. Doing what I could, I lovingly helped my sons behaviorally at home and supported teachers' accommodations in their classrooms. I also felt an inner resolve to accept my situation, knowing I was called to learn and practice bravery that was unconditional and unstoppable. Diligent with full awareness, it became its own reward. Paying attention to my own desires, cravings, experiences, and tendencies, I didn't *react* to them as much. When I was fully alert and grounded, I achieved an aliveness that felt freeing and discerning, making me more graceful and strong. I became less judgmental of myself and others because with greater awareness I also had more compassion.

Cultivating consciousness in your whole being may be challenging, but it reinforces itself. The more you do it, the more you want to. Increased connection with yourself helps you feel more self-love, safer, and empathy kicks in too. When you live moment to moment in this awake manner, you can more easily access the clear mind and full heart needed to stride into bravery in any given situation, then do what's best. Of course, this takes time and perseverance. Fully present, though, you'll be more spatially aware of everything going on and learn more quickly.

BRAVERY KEY: CHOOSING TO CONSCIOUSLY CREATE WHOLE-BEING AWARENESS WITH FULL CLARITY AND UNDERSTANDING, YOU WILL BE ABLE TO BROADEN YOUR REPERTOIRE OF RESPONSE CHOICES, ROUSING THE BRAVERY YOU NEED.

Try using the whole-being scan for a week, checking in multiple times each day. Whole-being awareness is a crucial component of developing the intrinsic bravery you want in the middle of adversity. You'll become a better parent, partner, friend, and leader. In the next chapter, "Now, There's This," you'll learn to assertively surrender to what *is* in any moment, even when adversity has landed.

CHAPTER 7

"Now, There's This":
Assertively Surrender to the Moment

"As you walk, eat and travel, be where you are. Otherwise you will miss most of your life."
— Jack Kornfield

Transformation begins inside the cocoon of the moment when we partner with the present.

Yet how do we handle the crises that keep coming our way when we love someone with addiction hurdles, with all the heartbreak and exhaustion we feel from their relapses, varied treatments, financial troubles, chaos, missed holidays, car accidents, disappearances, arrests, sorrow, regret, desperation, and overdoses? How do we manage the engulfing waves of our own helplessness when our beloveds struggle with panic attacks, anxiety, depression, altered states, off-the-charts ADHD, obsessive-compulsions, or devastating highs and lows? They may even have a combination of these two agonizing struggles, mental health *and* substance abuse challenges, painfully self-medicating with drugs or alcohol as flawed coping mechanisms for emotional health issues.

The Power of Assertive Surrender

In previous chapters we've learned about the four pillars in bravery training: befriending our feelings, using conscious breathing, becoming comfortable with discomfort, and knowing our true essence. Living with whole-being awareness helps us embed them and tune into what's happening. Another pivotal concept we must *integrate* to ingrain our courageous intentions and stand committed on a brave foundation is to surrender assertively into the new moment. Assertive surrender is a component of being fully present in this new now. It's an alchemical shift in our attitudes and actions from the resistance of "No, not that!" to an acceptance of "Okay, now, there's this." In doing so, we give up fights we can't win with the inevitable, which is already here.[29]

When I've been hit with tough news, I can't just suddenly "alter my mindset" and find relief or snap my fingers and begin to "think positively" about how hard experiences come with lessons I need to learn. The light may accompany the dark, but I've got to use a memorable concept or tool that helps me get to where I can bring myself into this new now with greater calm. On the journey of loving someone with mental and behavioral difficulties, I need techniques that are precursors to accepting what *is* so I can bring myself into this challenging moment with authenticity, fierce strength, and tender openheartedness.

Let's break it down into two steps:

1. The "now" part is about becoming present with whole-being awareness and surrendering to what *is* with dignity. By returning to presence, we become soothed a bit. Right here, right now, we accept that this is a brand new moment. And we're letting go of the past minute, the previous hour, and the day before when things were different.

2. "There's this" is about seeing the new circumstance which has arrived with eyes wide open, receiving it for what it is. Something is here now that we didn't want or ask for, and we can't go back in time. Wishing for anything other than what we've been delivered doesn't do any good and only creates more suffering on top of what just landed. Remembering we're here to grasp valuable lessons and

---

29   I heard about the concept of "Now, there's this" from Holly, one of my favorite yoga instructors, in one of her classes in Colorado Springs.

become brave, we let go of clinging to what isn't anymore. Both the suddenness and uniqueness of this particular arrival are part of our learning! We breathe a bit easier, release what was, and inhale what *is*. "Now, there's this" is an application of whole-being awareness. It is part of how we use our whole beings to fully tap into any moment.

Assertive surrender to the now is a very strong stance. We rise, openly awake, vulnerably strong in our bare skin, when we can say and live the concept of "Now, there's this." Who *wants* to yield though, right? We're taught that surrender is defeat. However, it's just the opposite. Bowing to our circumstances is a dignified honoring of what has now been presented. With our whole beings, we breathe into the moment, arrive fully in our bodies and hearts and recommit to radically accepting what *is*, just for now. If we resist and try to fight it, we will lose! Yet this moment won't last. Things change in every moment and will most certainly be different in a month, or a year. In the last chapter, we learned how we can handle the most excruciating discomfort and pain. We're not defined by past moments, but what we *do* in the present moment becomes embedded in who we are becoming. Soon enough, we'll know what has to be done. Yet, unless we unify with what *is*, our reluctance will influence our thoughts and actions negatively. Living with a "Now, there's this" approach is a way to find flow and create our own present story, without being influenced by our stories from the past or our fears about the future.

Radical Acceptance

I'm still learning how to practice this radical "Now, there's this" approach too! Recently I received another shocking phone call. In the middle of my clinical workday, at 1:00 p.m., a lead therapist at my son's dual diagnosis residential treatment program phoned to tell me that my son needed a higher level of care and must be transported from their facility by 7:30 that night! I immediately felt panic and confusion. I said, "I hear you, but there's no way I can get there before 7:30 p.m. tonight." Then he actually said, "We're kicking him out at 7:30. You can come get him or you can hire a sober transport, and I'll give you a name." His words stung and his attitude literally felt like a punch in my gut.

We live two hours from where my son was in treatment. I became furious at not knowing their policy about abrupt mental health escalation and discharge and how this particular man had spoken to me. Other centers I was aware of had various alternative protocols for de-escalation and transfers. I knew that my son's altered state had been escalating, but what had happened so suddenly today? I was told he was responding to a lot of internal emotional stimuli (also called psychosis), he was saying and doing odd things in the groups with other guys that made them very uncomfortable, and he'd even tried to get out of a moving car. He'd remained clean and sober, but his mental health issues had now become unmanageable. I asked why they couldn't just allow him to be safely isolated overnight for his sake (and that of the sober community) so that we could get there and make things happen in the morning. However, my words fell on deaf ears; they had their policy, and the caller wasn't budging. Everything I'd hoped for had suddenly and drastically changed. My son and I wanted and expected this program to be his last stop on the long road to his recovery. It *now* wasn't going to be. His mental health needs had unexpectedly risen above everything. Amid the scrambling, I paused and remembered how much I despised feeling this chaotic way and needed to operate from a place of clarity and calm. I breathed consciously and grounded down, feeling my feet connecting with the floor. Out loud, I said, "Now, there's this." I recommitted to trusting the process and actually bowed, honoring the moment.

The man hadn't offered empathy and refused to shift his position. The compassion I needed and longed for came from inside of me through conscious breaths. He gave me three names of higher-care programs and told me he'd present them to my son as well. We agreed that my son had the agency to choose and that we'd connect in an hour regarding his decision so that I could make plans to secure his placement. My attitude shifted further as I acknowledged and accepted what was happening. Breathing consciously, honoring my feelings, I stayed with the discomfort of this new now. Everything I knew to do started coming together. I slowed down, connected with my essence, and felt a wave of peace come over me. My whole being felt lighter and more held together, supported in the expansive zone of the now.

The "Now, there's this" approach of acceptance enabled my husband and I to drop everything and do what was needed in only a few hours. We knew that fighting the process would negatively impact all of us. The therapist called back an hour later with my son's choice. We made hotel arrangements for that night, flight arrangements for the next day, packed and headed out the door two hours later to drive to his center and pick him up. Whole-being awareness and acceptance of this new now productively played out continuously into the night and throughout the next day.

Surrendering assertively to the now, my understanding and compassion for both my son and this therapist broadened. The therapist rightly felt he had to protect his sober community and believed that moving my son on to a better placement had to happen quickly. Seeing and accepting what *is* turned out to be empowering, a form of radical acceptance.[30] I continued to relax into this new now, and my cognitive capacity returned. When my son called us along our drive to pick him up that evening, we encouraged him to talk candidly with the placement person at the new program. He felt our positive energy, our faith in him and the process, and phoned the intake person for his interview. That night when we picked him up, he said that this was a more equipped placement for him anyway, and he was excited to go. He knew the higher-care program had more to offer him and was ready to commit to it for three months. We shared many smiles and hugs that evening.

Ideally, in the addiction treatment world, I would have been notified in a more timely and gentle manner that they were discharging him so that both he and I could properly prepare for such an immediate and drastic

---

30   Tara Brach teaches about the term "Radical Acceptance" and wrote a book on the subject, *Radical Acceptance*. See Ram Das, *Be Here Now*, and Eckhart Tolle, *The Power of Now*.

change. However, the reality is, we don't live in that ideal world. So, in order to manage these kinds of sudden shifts, we can use a "Now, there's this" approach, as I did in this situation, to do what was ultimately best for my son.

Now, There's This = Awareness —> Adaptability—> Resilience

How do you embody this concept of surrendering to the moment? You *believe* in it because you feel better when you partner with the new now. You *commit* to living with flow, rolling from moment to moment, awake from dawn until dark. A conscious, aware approach of whole-being openness to what *is* leads to greater adaptability, then to resilience, which is positively *reinforcing*. "Now, there's this" is a motto and a mantra. Living in the moment, you rediscover the kindness of *presence*, which is perhaps the most enlightened way to live, and conscious bravery requires it.

This is much easier said than done. Sometimes I experience dissociation. You may too. I call it fuzziness in the moment, feeling like I'm not really all there. It's been an automatic mechanism my body has used to cope periodically since I was a teenager, a result of trauma I didn't know how to handle any other way. However, in this new now, having learned to engage my loving essence with whole-being awareness, I am able to find soothing presence. By combining conscious breathing, allowing feelings and discomfort with self-empathy, I soon receive inner reassurance. Things will be as they will be. They may be okay or not. I'll proceed, with the amount of bravery I've got at the time. It requires commitment and tenacity to reset repeatedly. With practice at being present day in and day out, I gain dexterity. Just as staying with discomfort is agonizing, surrendering to the moment can be arduous work in bravery training. Occasionally, dissociative numbness or tremendous sadness or anger might accompany my choice, so it may feel more wrong than right. Relinquishing control, bowing to wisdom, can be like that.

Holding the White Flag with Dignity and Grace

The rewards are many: We make better choices, feel capable as we take next steps, and can even find some humor and smiles along the way. We're not as easily overtaken with depression or panic, as self-empowerment emerges from within us. Over the years, there are days when I've surrendered well, and times I've given in while kicking and screaming. The former is much more rewarding. Metaphorically, when I've held the white flag while standing tall with dignity and grace, even when it hurt, I've regained my strength and manifested bravery in small and big ways. Periods when we are suffering are the most powerful opportunities to hone this skill.

"Now, there's this" is another way of choosing to radically accept what *is* for the time being. It takes faith to have long-term endurance and vision, rebalancing during the tough moments we'd rather run from. Boldly taking small steps into the unknown, we respectfully honor the onset of change with either daring activation, gracious surrender, or both.

> **BRAVERY KEY: WITH A "NOW, THERE'S THIS" APPROACH, WE ACCEPT OUR SITUATION WITH CONFIDENCE AND DIGNITY, APPRAISE IT, AND ASSERTIVELY SURRENDER GRACIOUSLY TO IT. AFTER PAUSING TO REGAIN PRESENCE, WE CAN THEN TAKE THE MOST APPROPRIATE NEXT STEP, MOVING WITH WHAT *IS* INTO BRAVE ACTION.**

In the next chapter, we'll maintain our capacity to be present while we learn how asking for help is an important component of both presence and bravery.

CHAPTER 8

Ask for Help: Seek Refuge

"Just because you are soft doesn't mean you are not a force. Honey and wildfire are both the colour gold."
—*Victoria Erickson*

Shocking news tears holes in the fabric of our days. Hearing that our beloveds have fallen into depression or have relapsed, it's all too easy to fall and break ourselves. When we're in a crisis, it's hard to be brave alone. There's no shame in asking for help when we feel weak or need fresh ideas. There is strength in reaching out, and that strength comes in numbers. Asking for and receiving aid are critical skills in cultivating courage.

Repeated tumultuous mental health circumstances create more than deep emotional, physical, and soulful heartache. These repeated experiences oftentimes freeze us up in isolation. It's easy to become desperate during such periods, feeling alone in the wilderness when addicted beloveds lose their spirit, relapse, or get arrested. Heartbroken, we long for someone to listen, to feel, and to understand our pain. Yearning for guidance, it's important to find and cultivate resources to assist in developing better coping mechanisms.

However, asking for help can be difficult because we feel so naked, so exposed. Often, trying to manage alone, we forget that all are woven together in a supportive, loving web, not meant to undertake life in solitude. As beings who are part of a human system, we're in an intricate network of beautiful connectivity. What a gift it is if only we can remember this and vulnerably tap into the power available by uniting with others during crises. Finding refuge can save us. Other people warm us up, and we rise up, out of the cold, lonely darkness. Not only do we feel their love and soothing, but by asking for and joining with the wisdom and guidance of others, we have the ability to access our inner power as well.

What does help really look like? It's when we're empowered by the assistance we receive from both the potency of our invincible human spirit and the powerful, mystical energy of our never-ending universe. Requesting help isn't simply making a phone call to a friend; it's linking arms with mystery. We receive support and consolation from the miraculous power of *love* that forms galaxies, saves lives, and transforms evil. With all this combined help, we know we're not alone.

The Power of Boundless Support

What does support look like, and how does it assist us? In our day-to-day experience, help can come to us in several different ways. Consider these four ways:

First: Supportive help is *sacred listening*, which is the experience of authentic connection, deep empathy, and validation. Being heard by someone who is fully present with us in genuine caring is a form of compassionate attention—a true gift of help. Because sometimes all we really need is for someone to listen, someone whom we know genuinely cares and supports us. It is healing in and of itself to be heard without feeling judged. In fact, crying uncontrollably as someone upholds us is also sacred. Their unconditional kindness provides solace as we feel understood and even guided.

Second: Help is someone *holding space for us* in our pain without judgment. They sit with us, physically, mentally, and emotionally engaged. With them fully focused on us, we feel safe expressing our feelings and are richly consoled.[31] A solid and even mystical exchange occurs between us, and another with their unconditional presence.

Third: In receiving validation and support for our intimate feelings from

---

31 "What 'Holding Space' Means Plus Five Tips to Practice," gstherapycenter.com.

someone who meets our needs, aid arrives via *brainstorming together*, incorporating their ideas, knowledge and wisdom as specific resources available to us.

Fourth: Giving and receiving help is a loving exchange of energy that *links us with the infinite unity* of the entire universe. Everything is interconnected.

Believing we are alone in our struggles is an illusion. When we return to presence and connect on a heart and soul level with another, knowing we are all intertwined, we realign with the Divine. In openly receiving or giving help, there is a sense of support from what is truly boundless, the limitlessness of something greater, which is our deepest force for aid and strength. Isn't this amazing? Knitted tightly in togetherness, we find sweet reprieve from our sense of aloneness.

There's immeasurable, undefinable energy at work in all things, a design we might not understand, where the potent power of banding together gives us indescribable relief. Sometimes there's nothing that can be done immediately in certain situations other than to be present and wait it out. Yet when our raw emotions are heard and felt by someone holding space for our aching, we can carry on and be braver, knowing that Divine power and mystery sustain us too.

Cultivating Authentic Connections

Cultivate authentic connections early on, when things are calm, so you're not waiting until the last minute. Have team players already lined up and ready to go when adversity hits. To construct a community of co-seekers, look for people like yourself who are finding their own way while supporting a loved one with addiction and mental health issues at the same time. Connecting with people who understand what you're going through with your loved ones and are not judgmental of their challenges or uniqueness is crucial. We need to come together not just for support but to also speak up and break stigmas individually and collectively.

For both the easier times and the devastating ones, I have four professionals and a mentor as my anchors who understand that mental health issues are family undertakings, not solely the challenge of any individual. You, too, will want the comfort and ideas from experienced psychotherapists, boundaries coaches, support groups, and mentors with a family-systems approach. Find one or two with the outlook on addiction, substance abuse, and behavioral health that aligns with you. Their healing ears, eyes, and hugs will sustain you. Their warm caring is a type of sanctuary from the cold.

Just as important are trusted friends, family, and colleagues. Feeling held, treasured, contained and/or supported by someone you genuinely love creates an alchemical shift from the wreckage of a crisis into the possibility that somehow mending can occur. Unforeseen magic and even seeming miracles happen in your authentic connections. David Whyte talks about friendship as witness, of "being seen by someone and the equal privilege of being granted the sight of the essence of another."[32] Loving friends remind you that you are not just a person going through a tough time; they also see you for who you have been over the years. The privilege of being seen and seeing others sometimes arrives uncomfortably in your world in the middle of tragedy.

You may also want to turn to the internet for trusted allies. It's easier now to connect with others on video chats than ever before. Your way finders are not just local; they're all around the globe.

Cohesive Synergy

The art of creating a team is a synergistic skill. You design your unique tribe and create powerful, authentic allies. Linking arms with others in synergy, you're much stronger and more capable of taking on pain and discovering solutions. Reach out to find your people. If you feel like you don't have any, look for a few of them. You're not alone, and you're valuable. Practice remembering your value and courageously connect instinctually as you form a cohesive pack. Sometimes it does take a tribe!

---

32   David Whyte, *Consolations*.

In cohesiveness, you summon others to pitch in and help mend your wounds. The word "cohesive" comes from the Latin word *cohaerere*, which means "to cleave together." When things are cohesive, they are unified and stick together. You don't have to do this alone! Team up with people to explore options and flesh out what's needed through back-and-forth conversations. Refuge arrives through other people, reinforcing your ability to work with them and stick together in cohesive synergy. As a result, you find a safe place to land.[33]

Seek out synergistic cohesion by seeing it as a gift to yourself, viewing it through the lens of self-care as opposed to losing or gaining control. Replace limited, unworkable beliefs, such as, "I've got to carry my own cross," or "I made my bed; now I have to lie in it." Remember, you are valuable and deserve to seek out the gift of collaboration. Bravely shift worn-out perspectives, motivating yourself by embedding new beliefs that sustain you, such as, "It's strong to ask for help," "I am one with others," and "I stick with my tribe." Get motivated to be brave here, remembering that courage requires daring. Rise up and make lists of people to contact, then push send on a text or email. It's hard, but you can do hard things.[34] You learn how by doing them.

Heroines and Heroes

I'm a big believer in heroines and heroes. Others who've walked similar paths to mine have kept a steady pace, persevered, and thrived—people who serve as role models for me, showing how they found their own way through the muck so I could follow in their footsteps. My favorite brave champions during the toughest times have been archetypal guides for me; characters in books and films like Harry Potter; Eowyn in *The Lord of the Rings*, and Katniss in *The Hunger Games* where, against all odds, these protagonists rose from impossible situations. How did they do it? With help. Think about it. Superheroes don't make miracles happen on their own; they always discover the need for a crew of other people on their

---

33   Sara Bareilles's song, "A Safe Place to Land."

34   Glennon Doyle.

team. My heroines and heroes in the realms of addiction and mental health are many, and I value their varying perspectives and research, including David Sheff, who wrote *Beautiful Boy* (which is now a major motion picture),[35] Gabor Mate,[36] Sandra Swenson,[37] Russell Brand,[38] Brad Reedy, Glennon Doyle,[39] Xavier Amador,[40] Kevin McCauley,[41] Denise Dryden,[42] Dai Kato,[43] and Erica Spiegelman.[44]

Expand your pool of resources to include a hero or two, role models who have come out of the fire, not just standing but as blazing examples. Miracles and magic occur when you combine forces.

Don't Wait

Becoming irrationally angry at yourself when you "need" help, you may sometimes use the word "admit," as if admitting you desire aid is a flaw, a fault, or a weakness. Don't be so hard on yourself! There's freedom in overriding views taught by our society to be self-sufficient and independent. You can decide to reprogram beliefs, understanding that others can help you locate a compass. Don't wait for negative consequences to force you to see "I can't do this on my own." It's both raw and strong to acknowledge "I need help," as your voice cracks and tears stream down your face.

Many people unfortunately wait too long before asking. Instead of

---

35   David Sheff, *Beautiful Boy* and *Clean*. Founder of Beautiful Boy Fund to end addiction: www.beautifulboyfund.org. The fund "is devoted to making quality, evidence-based care available to people suffering from problems related to drug use and addiction and identifying and supporting research to further the field of addiction medicine."

36   Gabor Mate, "Best Explanation of Addiction"; I highly recommend this YouTube video and his book, *In the Realm of Hungry Ghosts*.

37   Sandra Swenson, *Tending Dandelions*.

38   Russell Brand, *Recovery*.

39   Brad Reedy, *The Journey of the Heroic Parent* and *The Audacity to be You*.

40   Xavier Amador, "*I'm Not Sick, I Don't Need Help.*"

41   Kevin McCauley, "Pleasure Unwoven." (DVD).

42   This was recommended by my neighbor Kirsten, a true-life cat detective!

43   Denise Dryden, Integrational Wisdom, Whitefish, MT.

44   Erica Spiegelman, *Rewired*.

noticing what's happening in your breaking heart and body with tender, sharp-eyed observation, you may minimize or even ignore symptoms. Then they intensify, finally calling out to you in an emergency. You might often postpone going to a psychotherapist or calling in your tribe, until crisis hits. When you take a metaphoric leap off a burning building sooner rather than later, *before* a situation gets to the boiling point, you find there's a life net at the bottom. Wait too long and there's nothing but hard, unyielding pavement.

Sometimes, though, it feels frightening, almost impossible, to take that leap, or even keep going. A devastating event may have occurred in your own life on top of what your loved one was facing with their addiction and/ or mental health.

As an example: One spring a few years ago, in addition to the murky mess my sons were wading through, my soul pet of fifteen years passed away. Socrates, the wise cat. My beautiful Maine coon. He was so playful and sweet; each day we had rituals of silliness and loving connection. He was always present and dependable and had a sense about what I was feeling. As many of you know, our pets intuit us, and we have an intimacy that's indescribable. That was the bond we had. In his wildish instincts, he knew when things were awry. He was elated when I was joyous. I would often dance with him in my arms. He loved playing hide-and-seek together and never outgrew it over all those years. We shared an almost symbiotic relationship like no other I've ever known; he was a once-in-a-lifetime friend. Socrates had grieved with me when my previous husband passed away and when my sons were adrift. He'd moved with me to three different homes and navigated the displacement we experienced when we had to evacuate one of them during a fire in our city. He was adaptable and resilient.

Late one August night several years before Socrates passed, he got out of the house through a patio door that had accidentally been left open overnight. A thoroughly indoor cat, he had never been outside for more than a couple of minutes. I realized it the next morning and jumped into action, not waiting for him to turn up. My husband and I looked for him morning and night for three and a half weeks, holding flashlights at dusk and wearing headlamps in the early morning hours. Tuna was a rare treat for him, so I took a can with me daily as we searched up and down alleys and streets, calling out for him, "Socrates, tuna!" I taped over fifty bright yellow posters with huge color photos of him up on each corner stop sign nearby and delivered identical flyers to every mailbox for miles around, offering a reward for his return.[45] I asked that anyone who spotted him text or call me ASAP. Socrates was easily identifiable because he was a unique looking, beautiful, large cat with long, thick hair and a big bushy tail. I loved him and he loved me, and I was not going to give up on him, especially when I couldn't control what was happening simultaneously with my sons. Because I asked for help immediately, our whole neighborhood came together in the search to locate him, and people stopped by our home day after day with reports of seeing him on their property or streets. He was moving north and was seen getting water from two neighbors' koi ponds. I kept searching because people continued to text me that they'd caught a glimpse of him on the run.

Finally, on the afternoon of a birthday party I was having for my husband, neighbors over a mile away saw him dash under their porch and came to my house to tell me in person. My friend and I grabbed his crate and a can of tuna, and we drove like lightening over to their home. Socrates was lying under their porch ten feet away and meowed at me, but seemed full of fear. I opened the can of tuna, which lured him close to us, shaking; but before taking a bite, he turned and scootched back into hiding. I called him again and again, "Socrates, tuna," putting some fish in the dish I'd brought along. He came close again. We grabbed the scruff on his neck and pulled him out. I held him close and cried with relief. He was all bones; he'd lost five and a half pounds. We got him to the vet just in time to save his life.

Over two hundred people in our neighborhood collectively came together to help me find Socrates. I counted all the calls and texts I'd received, and all the people who had spoken to me on the street. I got to

---

45   Dai Kato, holistic therapist, SMART therapy, Boulder, CO.

know my community that August because of Socrates. Over seventy-five different people wrote about him in our online newsletter chat, coming together in unity over this experience that most everyone could relate to, of losing and finding a dear pet. One man even wrote a wonderful short story about him that everybody raved about. Our local association dedicated the month of August to him, "Socrates, the Cat Who Lived."

I knew Socrates by heart. I knew him and he knew me. I knew his scent, smelled and felt him upon awakening, picked him up and snuggled him throughout the day, and slept with him at my feet. I was his and he was mine. Four years after he was lost then found, Socrates died. His death knocked me off my feet for three months. Because my sons had pulled away and were overtaken by the beast of addiction at that time, when Socrates passed, the abrupt absence of my soulful constant left me feeling even more alone and despairing. With the double-edged sword of grief for my absent sons and darling companion, I lost focus, lost productivity, and lost sleep. So that I didn't also lose my will, I called my life coach. The logical part of me was saying, "He was a pet. This grieving process shouldn't be overtaking me." But I cried my heart out to her, sobbing. It was one of three times in my life I've actually wailed in mourning. Sometimes she just listened, and her silent, loving partnership upheld me in refuge and gave me courage.

Her strong comfort was soulfully nurturing. I spoke of the losses that were all culminating, how I was afraid for my sons to be injured or die from their drug use. Every fear was coming up for me all at once, and I felt despair. But my coach understood and reminded me how Socrates had consoled me in my darkest moments. He'd been with me through everything, all the most blissful times and the deepest sorrows. She told me, "He was your constant soul friend. He's been with you through every tragedy for almost fifteen years. If you can get through this, you'll be able to get through anything." And I knew that was true. With her counsel, I found a safe place to land and moved through this complex loss over time. Fully allowing the grief over my sons being gone and caught up in their whirlwinds of drug use, I learned how to pull together everything I knew about becoming brave. I grew more tenacious than I ever knew I could be.

Just as importantly, unforeseen help came to my aid. The same can be true for you when you don't wait and ask for help.

One Impossible Step at a Time

We don't have the luxury of despair.[46] Our beloveds need us to be strong and brave. They also need us to help them break the addiction and mental health stigmas we share in this world, and further research in these fields.[47] Yet, proceeding forward can feel like finding our way at night through a dark, unfamiliar home. Discovering that others are there with us, the collaborative alliance reorients us and shines a light. One seemingly impossible step at a time, we link arms and begin. Starting with undertaking "what's necessary, we then do what's possible, and suddenly (we) are doing the impossible." (Francis of Assisi) Mustering the voice to ask, reach out for support and seek refuge during these hardships; our sense of safety and hope increases when we receive it. A motion-sensor light turns on, and we realize we're not alone in the house. Cracking our hearts wide open as we request that someone give us a hand is one of the bravest and most vulnerable things we can do. It makes it easier to seek reinforcement the next time.

When we sit together in shared anguish with a person we care about, a solid and even mystical exchange occurs between us with our unconditional, loving presence. We all need somebody to lean on. Showing each other what our immense capacity for conscious bravery looks like, we walk into the wilderness with it, together.

BRAVERY KEY: IT'S STRONG, WISE, AND BRAVE TO ASK FOR HELP. DON'T BE A SOFT FORCE. JOIN FORCES.

No longer feeling as alone or lost, you can trust yourself and this

---

46   Cheryl Strayed, *Tiny Beautiful Things*.

47   Regarding support and research, there are dozens of people and groups to choose from, so I've listed a few recommendations under "Resources." With tribes who understand the complexities of neurodiversity and addiction, sensitive crews of people working together with us in a positive, sacred approach to giving and receiving, we all thrive because we truly are in partnership.

unpredictable process. In the next chapter, you will learn how to listen to your fear as an adviser amid the unknown.

CHAPTER 9

Fear as an Adviser

"We're all afraid. We just have to get to the point where we understand it doesn't mean that we can't also be brave."
—Brene' Brown[48]

Perhaps the most unnerving, daunting force humans face is fear. Startling the body into alarm with paralysis, shouting, crying, bolting, shaking, or recoiling, fear is both an emotion and a full-on experience. It's a reaction that will pass, but often seems as if it's an entity of its own that will remain indefinitely. Fear has might and potency because it is often accompanied by a larger range of other feelings: shock, anger, sadness, even disturbance or disgust. It can be especially overwhelming because fear is the voice calling out alerts about devastating occurrences which cause accompanying pain and immobilization.

Fear grew tougher over time as thousands of years molded it into a biological process. Connected to the autonomic nervous system, fear is in control of sending survival alerts in bursts of energy to the whole being, commanding fight, flight, or freezing to achieve safety. Humans have unfortunately evolved to hear its voice as menacing, view it as an enemy, cower under its shadow, inclined to sprint away from its forceful shrieks, or feel an urge to raise fists, readying for combat. Remembering fear long after the event that caused it reinforced fear of fear itself.[49]

---

48   Brene' Brown, "You Might Be Afraid and Not Even Know It," on SuperSoul Sunday with Oprah, YouTube.

49   Franklin D. Roosevelt, "The only thing we have to fear is fear itself."

You can't live without fear because it is a warning signal coming from your brain stem; it's built into how you function and survive. Fear's intent is to call out danger warnings in your service, and its job is to protect you, demanding you pay attention to something risky or threatening with its alerts. To be certain, fear has an alarming voice, but it speaks words of warning that need to be heard.

Fear as an Adviser

An outlook shift helps you work with your body's programming. What you *believe* about fear can enable you to manage it. Changing your perspective by altering old, worn-out beliefs is critical. You may have historically viewed fear as disabling or seen it as an *enemy* to overcome. These are limited beliefs which keep you stuck, without capacity to hear the advice of what fear has to offer or respond with bravery. Instead, make a conscious shift to recognize fear as one of many advisers with whom you consult.

Fear is mostly impartial. However, it has a good memory and recalls things that have hurt you, traumatized you, triggered, or stirred you up. Its announcements come from a database of information about you. Since it knows so much about you, place fear in an advisory role and listen to what it has to say—among your other consultants in bravery training, like love, kindness, sadness, anxiety, and despair. All these emotions and experiences have something to say to you, so learn to listen to each of them without getting wedged in a rut by listening to any one of their voices incessantly. When you're able to view fear as an adviser, you'll consider its cautions, reflect, then move forward with small, courageous steps. Like a good friend whose counsel has been taken, fear will feel validated, its loud voice will quiet, and you become clear about what to do next.

Less Fearful but Not Fearless

Fearlessness is unwise. The fearless are likely to get into accidents by not watching for traffic properly or making poor choices because they falsely believe negative consequences won't follow. You need to listen to fear as your adviser rather than being fearless, thereby going about your business with *discernment*.[50] Try to release the pressure to be completely brave, and simply fear less. You'd be in danger more often if fear didn't warn you. Since the intent behind fear is to help keep you safe, by knowing fear's good intentions, you listen to its warnings as potentially helpful information to ward off a possible dire situation. You become *less fearful* but not fearless.[51]

Calming Down

Fear can freeze you up in stomach-churning fixations about your loved one, obsessions about their well-being, and a sense that you need to solve their problems for them. It can cloud your mind and heart, draining optimism and hope. It's important to be able to calm yourself down and develop a *responsive but not reactive* relationship with fear's felt threats so that you are more prepared to handle the worst with an embedded capacity to respond proactively. If you've never really listened to fear, you may not know how to hear or heed its advice. Calm your body and heart down first by conscious breathing to override automatic instincts that want to mute fear. You can then hear what it's saying. When you have a couple of minutes, take these steps to calm down:

Breathe consciously. Do everything you know about honoring this feeling so that you can listen more closely to what it's trying to tell you than to the body's response.

Listen to what you're afraid of. Identify your fear. Say "I am afraid of _____." Accept it. Honor it.

Ground down. Anchor your feet and notice what's happening in your body. If some part of your body hurts, like your stomach, your heart, your throat, or the top of your head, place a hand there in acknowledgment and soothing.

Give yourself empathy and love. Whatever is causing your fear feels

---

50   Elizabeth Gilbert, *Big Magic*.

51   Ryan M., Yoga class themed on bravery, "Core Power on Demand."

daunting to face. Close your eyes for just a moment and keep breathing with whole-being awareness, bringing compassion to yourself (and the other person involved, if possible) while continuing to use conscious breaths through an open mouth. Surround your energy bubble with empathy coming in, and loving-kindness going out. Thank your intuition for coming in to help you now as well.

Find safety. Do what it takes to feel as safe as you can, as quickly as you can. Wrap a soft blanket around yourself, drink some warm tea, or go stand outside and look at the sky. Do something that's fresh and comforting, bringing renewal into your world after the scary event or news.

Move your body! You do this naturally in any trauma response, so initiate it consciously. Stand if you can; shake your arms, hands, and head. Bounce and kick your legs. Remove the heaviness, as if you're shaking snow off your whole body! Now with the weight lifted, you can listen for the advice fear has to offer. Activating the capacity of your whole being to *shift*, fear will feel heard and quiet down.

If you don't have time for the whole process, at the minimum try to breathe consciously and get grounded. You'll discover more control if you can *respond* to fear's warnings with empathy and love, shaking it off instead of *reacting*.

Know Your Triggers

Triggers are a person's unique emotional reactions to troubling, provocative, or disturbing content, based on their own past experiences. To prepare for fear's arrival, know your triggers and know what you're afraid of so that you're ready when fear announces that one of them is impending. You're then better able to put things into perspective and tend to the actual situation without overreacting and being overwhelmed by it. For example, you may be afraid your loved one will not become independent and will always need your help. Knowing you're worried that they won't develop into capable adults once you're gone helps you see the importance of doing what you can now, supporting them in establishing important life skills.

When alerted with news about a setback, you're able to compose yourself and address the situation with clarity and insight.

Research shows that people are more afraid of the unknown than of actual physical pain.[52] If this is true for you, fear of the unknown is a trigger to begin to work on. You may be fearful of your loved one's injury or death. Some of you may have loved ones who have prostituted themselves for drugs or have been physically and sexually assaulted by drug dealers. My sons and I have been through some of the most horrific trauma imaginable. Unfortunately, *trauma* is a major part of the addiction and mental health worlds. Navigating through this harrowing wilderness is part of why it takes every ounce of bravery you can muster and using the best techniques that you can find.

If you're scared, you may not only be afraid, you may also fear that things will get worse, or that you'll go down an undesirable, dark path you've been down before. You can become very fixated on not wanting things to get bad, but this overfocus can be the very thing that takes you down the rabbit hole. That can subconsciously cause you to go back into old, defective coping patterns which are then, ultimately, what end up sending you back to that unwanted place or keeping you there. Having awareness about what causes fear to get a grip on you, you're better prepared when it happens.

Control

Many people know they do not have control over their loved ones' mental health, drug or alcohol use and their circumstances. Yet, on top of that, they believe their fear is out of their control too. This is far from true, because dwelling in fright or panic brings added distress to those already managing the difficult situations encountered by a loved one who has unpredictable highs and lows, social isolation, or who needs intensive treatment. Frightening circumstances arrive all too often from these interwoven challenges of mental health and substance dependency. One can't control *when* the feeling of fear hits, but *altering beliefs about it*

---

52   Pema Chodron, "True Happiness" audio.

makes it more manageable to move through and past it when it does. Fear is nothing new for those here who are especially familiar with its frequent warnings on daily treks through this intimidating, unchosen, unpredictable wilderness. It becomes essential to learn how to manage being afraid in order to evoke daily courage and protect contentment.

Your loved ones suffer, and you can't prevent it or stop it. When you choose fear as an adviser, you are better prepared to be notified when your beloved incurs hardship. Making peace with the fact that they sometimes suffer means becoming less afraid. Able to view fright in a new way, you receive its news with pained receptivity instead of begrudging it. You need to move past the memories of fear and even terror you've experienced. Work consciously to move through them and acquire resilience. This journey you're on with your loved ones is long. It may even last a lifetime. Do more than trudge on; return to serenity and walk on a path of contentment by using techniques to manage your fear.

Fear is here to stay, *and* could arrive often. Be prepared to not let it immobilize you and leave you suffering. Allowing fear to become an adviser you've chosen to have on your team provides you with some control, and you're prepared to listen to its counsel when the inevitable calamities occur.

Terror, Trauma, and Grief

The drug world is a formidable place, and those in it can experience *terror, trauma, and/or grief.* The scope of these is too great to address in this book. Terror can be trauma inducing, and you may have night terrors, recurring nightmares, sleep disturbances, or frequent and overwhelming fear. Different people respond to similar situations with varying abilities to cope. Trauma is its own beast, so ask for help and work with a skilled trauma therapist if you're struggling to heal.

Grief is its own process, common for those who walk alongside someone with their own frequent losses. Watching your loved one fall, seeing their life threatened or even pass away is a topic that needs more attention than I can honorably give here. Additionally, you don't simply feel your own grief and confront trauma. It's common to experience vicarious trauma and grief, secondary to your loved ones' exposure. You may fear that you don't have the capacity to cope with these adversities repeatedly. Yet you must learn. Grief over the pain your loved ones face, coupled with trauma you go through alongside them, will likely continue. Addiction and mental health issues instigate unremitting and recurring losses and tragedies. You know the importance of receiving support—in self-kindness, prompt yourself to get it.

The Night They Came for Him

One terrifying summer night I was wearing all-white clothes. I rarely, if ever, dress that way. But for whatever reason I had on white pants, a bright white top, and cream sneakers. My youngest son had been told the day before by his public defender to stay out of trouble that weekend, with a court hearing coming up on Monday. My husband, son, and I had enjoyed a nice Saturday, going on a hike together earlier and grilling burgers on our patio. We'd eaten outside, with laid-back conversation. It was almost midnight, and I was reading in the living room while my son was up in his room. He came down from upstairs and said, "I'm meeting a couple of girls in a few minutes." Not wanting to boss a twenty-one-year-old but still needing to set boundaries, I said, "We've had a nice day. We agreed you were going to stay home. Just stay in, please." He replied, "I'll just sit in their car on the street with them. I'll come back in a half hour." And with that, he walked out the front door. Hmm, I thought. Fear sensors went up. Thinking he was clean at the time, I was afraid he'd be doing drugs again. But knowing he might just sit in their car to talk, I didn't want to micromanage. I just needed to know what was going on. Listening to fear's warning, I ran upstairs and watched my son from the guest room window. He was standing outside facing north, glancing from his phone to the street, waiting for the girls to arrive. But from the south, I saw a car creeping up the street with its lights turned off, slowly approaching our home. High alert from fear! I was afraid "they" were coming for him. Triggered, I immediately wanted to protect him. I ran down the stairs, shouted at my husband to call the police and dashed out the door. By then, my son was already running, and three men were chasing him. He darted into a neighbor's yard with all three guys still bolting after him. I quickly screamed, "Hey! Stop!" But all I could hear were muffled, rustling, and grunting sounds. These guys were beating my son up!

They'd left their dark convertible unattended, with the engine still running and the top down. So I stood next to it waiting for the police, fearing for my son's life but knowing I couldn't get involved in the fight. *Fear* told me what I *could do* was face them, take their photo, and try to scare them away. Heeding fear's advice, I nervously waited for their return. Noticing one of their phones left unattended on the car seat, fear's wisdom told me not to grab it so as not to instigate them further or get pulled into the chaos.

I heard angry voices talking. Only a minute later, three guys ran back toward their vehicle as fast as they could, but I was next to it, standing tall like a mama polar bear in white. I screamed at them, "Who are you people? We've already called the police!" I slammed the palm of my hand down on the hood of their vehicle. As they leaped back into their seats, I yelled, "They will find you!" I held up my phone to take their photo, while moving out of the way as they began to speed off. I snapped shots of their vehicle and license plate. I didn't know it yet, because everything happened so fast, but my son had gone back inside through the back door, and my husband was helping him. I found out later that they were drug dealers, and my son owed them money. He'd thought that the girls who had texted him were meeting him out by the sidewalk; instead, it was a trick.

Not knowing that yet, fear's wisdom told me the girls who were supposed to meet him might still show up, and I watched to see. Sure enough, a vehicle was approaching from the north, the very direction my son had anxiously awaited their arrival. I started walking straight down the street toward them. I could see two young women inside, and as they passed, it dawned on me that they *all* might have conspired together to set my son up. I stared the two women down and said loudly, "Don't ever come here again!" They heard me. I was protecting my son and my family, and fear helped me do it.

Adrenaline helped me through the initial terror, but once back inside the house, I suddenly felt more frightened. I ran inside, and my son stood up. We held each other for the longest time, with no words. Fear for him overtook me, along with deep sorrow and empathy. It was incomprehensible at that moment, and my thoughts questioned: *how had he ended up in this daunting world with drug dealers and brutal attacks?* I didn't have any answers. My husband, son and I just sat on the sofa, quietly holding space together, holding each other for a while.

One thing I reflected upon: It's the beast of addiction we're *all* fighting, and those three young men and the girls were under its tight grip as well. I hoped that somehow they would get treatment, not go to jail or prison. I took in the seriousness of the whole situation. My son, sitting next to my husband and me, was dabbing his face with hydrogen peroxide. We knew he felt scared and battered. As he was telling us that he "wasn't hurt badly" and was relieved he "hadn't been knifed," I knew he was minimizing things. But we could address that another time. For now, he needed safety and soothing. My husband and I gave him our empathy and love.

My husband consoled me separately, too, that night while we got ready for bed and shook off the experience as best we could. Giving and receiving healing empathy is part of how I could move forward, viewing fear as one of my advisers. When I took off my white clothes before bed that night, I noticed dirty patches on my top and a couple of blood marks. Facing fear can be messy.

Messy Grace

When you're brave, you keep learning while things are messy. You can't walk around wearing white and not become a bit grubby. Being family members and friends of loved ones in the trenches of pain and suffering means you get down in the dirt with them, vulnerably knowing you are part of their challenges *and* their solutions. More real and raw, you bravely remove your own blinders. You can remain graceful, and at the same time be a fierce force.

Fear is your necessary companion and a valuable consultant. View it this way and you won't be overtaken by it or let it dominate you. You can listen to its warnings and consciously bring it along with you as an adviser instead of trying to avoid or overcome it. See fear as one adviser to whom you listen among all the emotions that give you alerts on your journey. Cotravelers in the wilderness with your beloved, fear will guide you into strength.

BRAVERY KEY: FEAR IS AN ADVISER RATHER THAN AN ENEMY.

Walk into the unknown with its wise counsel instead of viewing it as an adversary.

Less fearful but not fearless, you can return to a foundation of happiness that needs to be protected with all you've got. The next chapter is about how to do just that.

CHAPTER 10

Protect Your Happiness

"If you follow your bliss, you put yourself on a kind of track that has been there all the while, waiting for you, and the life that you ought to be living is the one you are living. Wherever you are—if you are following your bliss, you are enjoying that refreshment, that life within you, all the time."

—Joseph Campbell

People who know how to return to love, protect their happiness, and follow their bliss are *genuinely joyous.*[53] True happiness is inner contentment through all things, even during adverse circumstances. When you cultivate a foundation of genuine happiness you can discover your bliss. Living from whatever brings you delight, you eventually experience more frequent and sustained joy. Joy is an exuberant, vibrant form of true happiness. Many moments of pure bliss will be enjoyed when you have built a strong foundation of contentment. Without this, you may laugh, but the pleasure is fleeting. You'll experience more frequent, pure, lasting joy when it's anchored in happiness. When happiness becomes the most important thing you live for and cultivate, you protect it like the treasure it is.

There is a Latin phrase which refers to an absolutely essential thing, a "sine qua non." Happiness is a sine qua non for those who face the disease of addiction in their family or love someone who suffers with their mental health. The happier you are, the more present, conscious, and attentive you can be to the needs of your struggling beloved, even if things feel out of

---

53   Marianne Williamson, *A Return to Love.*

your control. Find and protect your happiness for *you*. Even when you're despairing, allow yourself to desire bliss and you'll begin to create the *strength* to cultivate courage. Losing sight of your aspiration makes you prone to believing that circumstances and other people determine your serenity in life. They don't. Choosing happiness, *you* have control over your outlook.

Not only is cultivating true happiness important, it is also vital to *protect it with everything you've got* because living with contentment requires emotional tenacity. It demands discipline to practice all the components of happiness discussed in this chapter, and sometimes it will be hard. But keep going because the process is satisfying and the result is worth it: you will find your bliss and follow it.

The essential components of true happiness are pillars which will help you cultivate and safeguard it: gratitude, empathy, forgiveness, savoring pleasant moments, and returning to the sweet spot. You may already believe in and practice them. Yet to create and protect true contentment, *they must be used in tandem* to vitally equip you for any difficulty and experience bliss.

Gratitude

Gratitude is absolutely essential to protecting happiness because it contributes to healing pain and fosters enjoyment. Gratitude is the regular practice of purposefully and consistently paying attention to what *can* be appreciated and enjoyed, no matter how small. You might not be able to be grateful *for* everything. Rather, try to remain grateful *through* everything.[54] Sometimes gratitude shows up after a tough event later, when you choose to vulnerably accept the dark gifts that arrived. Keeping an open mind and heart, the silver lining shows up and you find gratitude for something— what you learned—that things turned out better than expected, or simply that you're still breathing. When grateful, you naturally feel more

---

54   David Stendl-Rast, "How to Be Grateful in Every Moment (But Not for Everything)." On Being with Krista Tippett Podcast. www.onbeing.org.

content, because gratitude brings with it a sense of capacity to find beauty in unforeseen places. Being thankful for not just what you have but for life itself delivers warmth and relief. The more you practice this type of vulnerable appreciation, you will notice that unexpected, pleasant results appear, and you return to happiness.

Practice gratitude diligently and often. Write in a gratitude journal, drink your coffee every morning saying gratitude prayers, or ask your family to share a sentence about what they're grateful for at dinner. Build gratitude into your life so thoroughly that it deepens your happiness. While you're likely facing something very difficult right now, dig deep and ask—can you stretch and find one thing you are grateful for?

Even when my sons and I were going through the toughest challenges, I could always be grateful that they might have another opportunity and that I was in their lives to love them through it. Although I feared for their lives at times, I was grateful for the moments and the ability to have faith, without focusing on something bad that could happen.

Empathy

With a grateful heart, you're able to have empathy. Ashok Bhattacharya, my friend and fellow psychotherapist, is a specialist in empathy. He defines it as: "trying to experience the mental, physical, social, and spiritual experience of another from their point of view, not yours. It requires, in its purest form, self-negation, where your experience may contaminate your appreciation of the other."[55] Empathy then, is taking off your shoes and walking in the shoes of another on *their* path, with soulful compassion for them and everything they face. Understanding that others have their own demons, with compassion for them and yourself, you can move into freedom that leads to happiness. There is still accountability, but feeling empathy leads you to an explanation of why someone may have acted a certain way, helping you to let go of pain and anger.

People in the addiction realm are on a harsh, formidable, even sometimes

---

55   Ashok Bhattacharya, MD. The Empathy Clinic, Canada.

terrifying ride. My sons and I are a part of that world as you and your loved ones may be too. Empathy for your own people swells, and you can then show kindness to those who live in that realm. With empathy and kindness for yourself and others, you build on the foundation of your happiness and extend a basis for forgiveness.

Forgiveness

When I forgave the drug dealers for beating up my son, I focused more on the deep empathy I felt for them rather than the threat they potentially posed. They were hurting and were probably on methamphetamines, desperate for money. I put myself in their shoes. Feeling into their pain, I let go of bitterness.

Forgiveness is a conscious decision to "cease to harbor resentment," feeling sorrow over the circumstance instead of rage."[56] Even though it may feel like forgiveness is undeserved, you're not excusing or condoning the action, nor are you obligated to restore the relationship to what it used to be. Moving beyond blame and bitterness, you stop justifying continued anger, taking the heavy burden off your shoulders to set it down and alleviate your own pain. When you forgive, you feel relief, and it frees the energy bond between you and another person. Others are then viewed more positively as humans who make mistakes, and the world is perceived as a safer place.

Aspects of forgiveness will come in their own time in stages without forcing them. Initially, leaving things alone for a while, you can postpone the final act of forgiveness until you're ready. Any steps toward forgiveness are helpful and begin to provide freedom. Once you've begun to forgive, you experience a lightness and a sense of liberation, because surrendering into forgiveness actually feels strong. You deepen and protect your happiness.[57]

Savoring Pleasant Moments

It is essential to "accentuate the positive…and latch on to the affirmative"

56, 57   Clarissa Pinkola Estés, *Women Who Run with the Wolves*.

in life, as you learn to live from happiness and follow your bliss.[58] Focusing on the good that has happened and drawing on that energy must take precedence over ruminating on memories of hardships. Individuals naturally savor pleasant moments all the time. A smell, a taste, or a sound can prompt a happy memory, and you relish it because your whole being is engaged and you want to saturate yourself in the memory. You soak in that moment for a short time and then return to the now, happier. One can also *consciously* savor pleasant moments and return to contentment. For example, if you're upset about your loved one's mental health, deliberately relishing a pleasurable memory like laughing with them can bring hope. You'll naturally expand your view of the circumstances, recalling the good as well. This helps build a sense of security and containment, realizing there isn't constant danger to look out for. Intentionally delighting in pleasurable memories is an important technique to practice and develop. This ensures that the negative experiences from the past don't dominate the present outlook on life and you can truly cultivate and protect your happiness.[59]

You may have been through some traumatic years, making it understandably easy to become jaded and fearful that some version of what happened before may occur again. With whole-being awareness, you can establish a habit of savoring moments as they happen and revisit them often, overriding the brain's tendency toward negativity.[60] Thus, saving moments to cherish is a helpful tool reminding you to believe you can do a brave thing rather than fearing a repeat of a past time when you didn't.

I like to collect my pleasing moments now and then by pretending to string them up one by one on an imaginary strand of lights with other lovely moments. In my mind's eye, I suspend happy, soothing memories together on this light string, adding to them over the years as I commit to reflecting on them often. When I'm blue, I will place a savored moment next to a painful moment. It's a way to reduce the potency of a stinging

---

58   "Accentuate the Positive," song by Johnny Mercer and Harold Arlen.

59   Deb Dana, *Polyvagal Exercises for Safety and Connection*.

60   www.verywellmind.com for "Negative Bias Definition."

memory by rewiring the brain, bringing my mind and heart back into a place of optimism and faith. Stringing up nice moments like lights to guide me in the dark times enhances happiness.

Tap into one or more specific pleasurable memories then thread them together and line them up like little lights in your mind's eye. Here are the two simple steps: After noticing an upsetting memory, *first* accept that it has arrived and tend to it. See the image, allow the ache to emerge, and console your feelings. Recognize and label any accompanying longings, worries, fears, or challenging emotions. For example, you might say to yourself, "This still hurts so badly." From your commitment to become braver, the *second* step is to access a counter memory. Saturate yourself in a memory of connection, love, kindness, strength, gentleness, success, or empowerment. This makes you feel safe, connected, more positive, optimistic, and braver. Place that memory on your secured strand of multiple lights. Training the brain to reflect upon pleasant memories rewires it to focus upon safety versus danger and optimism versus negativity. Greater joy and bliss emerge in your life.

Howling with My Pack

A couple of years ago on a warm autumn night, I was at a friend's home. Five of us women were sitting in the near dark, lounging on her back deck around the fire pit, having great conversations. I almost didn't go because earlier that day I'd been panicked off and on, anxious about where my young adult sons' drug-influenced wanderings were taking them. It was a relentless, rough stretch for our family. Torn apart by both of them relapsing at once, I brought empathy to them, leading me into self-empathy. So, I opted for a choice to protect my happiness by getting together with some of my dearest friends.

My friend lived near the edge of our city, where bears and coyotes often wandered. Very close by, we heard the call of a coyote. It was met by an irregular unison of other coyote responses farther away. There was a long silence. We grinned and sat wide-eyed, looking at each other then out into the deep blue shadows. The lone coyote howled again. Without thinking,

I made an instinctual coyote call: "Ow-woooooo!" Silence. Then the lone coyote responded. We laughed. He thought I was a nearby buddy! He called again. I waited just long enough, then howled back. I was barely convincing this time, and he called once more. We giggled with delight. Then all of us howled in unison, but we sounded like an unpracticed orchestra, and knew it. No response from any of the coyotes. Laughing our heads off now, there was huge relief for all. I stayed present in the moment, grateful for having fun with a pack of my wild friends that night.

I felt an inner strength that helped me rise above pain and fears about my sons. It was a magical evening with lots of joyful moments that took the edge off my worries and helped me return to the concrete foundation of happiness that I protected well. There's a wildness to being whole, and that night I felt whole. Allowing myself these happy moments helped me override what might have felt deflating. I savored the evening and added the special moments to my string of lights.

The Sweet Spot

Happiness can also be cultivated by discovering and returning to the sweet spot. Finding the sweet spot is a way of reclaiming stability amid troubles that are rocking your world. It's like walking near the ocean: You find the sweet spot on the firm sand, between the two extremes of the unpredictable ocean and the deeper sand near land. Walking parallel to the water, if you move too close to the waves, water splashes on you. But if you walk farther away from the water, near the shore, the sand is deeper, making it hard to move forward. The ocean symbolizes feeling drowned by emotions, and the deep sand is when you're sinking, not getting anywhere. The sweet spot is where the sand is wet and packed.

In the past, during trying times when my sons were relapsing, it helped me to remember I could revisit that firmly grounded sweet spot within myself where there is a more solid foundation and greater ease. You can discover the sweet spot in your mind's eye by being aware of any situation's extremes and finding the middle path, where you're not feeling drowned by water or sinking in sand. The sweet spot is the only place on the beach where you'll leave defined footprints. It's easier to walk there on solid ground, not dragged down by your situation, as you carve your way through it all.

Guarding your happiness means consistently practicing gratitude, feeling empathy, offering forgiveness, delighting and savoring in pleasant moments and returning to the sweet spot. It doesn't hurt to howl a little too! Weave these essentials together, and you'll not only create happiness but also protect it with everything you've got.

BRAVERY KEY: PROTECT YOUR HAPPINESS AND YOU'LL EXPERIENCE BLISS.

All the components that create happiness lead you to the capacity for healthy self-care, which is discussed in the next chapter.

CHAPTER 11

Self-care: Be a Tall Tree

"People all over the world are starting to discover the joys of physical, emotional, and spiritual self-care. There is a universal hunger for change and enlightenment, and an end to unnecessary misery and suffering."
—*Erica Spiegelman, Rewired*

Self-care is a necessary luxury. It is your badge of honor, not sacrifice. You deserve self-care! It is not selfish. Selfishness is a disregard of others, whereas self-care is respectful regard for yourself.[61] Self-care is self-love in action, and it solidly supports research in not only protecting your happiness but in adapting to change and altering your life.[62]

Self-care is the mix of all the ingredients in the soup of "neuroplasticity": the brain's ability to rewire, alter perspectives, heal your whole being, remap behaviors, then grow and improve as a human.[63] Self-care is not only replenishing, it also creates new neural networks in the brain. Practicing behaviors that become habits and engaging in self-care *retrains your brain* to recover from challenges, prevent disease, and stockpile the abilities necessary to be a resource for your beloved. Just as eating a healthy meal cures being "hangry," you're better able to care for others when you've done something that is purely for yourself. It is renewing, energizing, and soulfully satisfying. And the benefits rub off on your loved one who watches your role modeling.

---

61   Demeter Delune, "Here's Why Self-Care is Not Selfish," www.medium.com.

62   Vanessa Loder, "How to Rewire Your Brain for Happiness," Forbes.

63   Courtney E. Ackerman, "What is Neuroplasticity?" www.positivepsychology.com.

Self-care is like drinking a glass of fresh spring water. When are you at your best during a stressful time? When you are feeling healthy and vibrant—often after you've rejuvenated with self-care. Taking good care of yourself, you are better able to take on the world, prepared to handle the adversities which will arrive in the sometimes-bumpy emotional life of your beloved. You become anti-fragile, which is even more robust than being resilient.[64] Caring for yourself is one thing you can change amid difficulties. Frame self-care in a way that makes you want to do it.

The Tree of Life

Self-care can bring you joy! Just like happiness, self-care is a sine qua non, an absolutely essential thing in order to be present for yourself and your loved one and your potential to develop antifragility and bravery.

You may feel so overwhelmed right now that it's hard to get out of bed or even smile, let alone think of self-care. Don't feel you have to do everything I'm suggesting here. I'm simply presenting various ways that self-care can look. Consider reading this chapter in sections if you feel the need. I encourage you to try one idea here today. As you're ready, choose something else, and in time, you'll be more motivated.

You know what it looks like to care for others and what that requires. But you may not be as good at taking care of yourself yet. To truly support your loved one, you must become a master at self-care. A beautiful image to remind you of self-care is the Tree of Life symbol. With this metaphor in mind, imagine yourself as being a tall tree, deeply rooted with a thick, sturdy trunk of protection from the elements. Your healthy branches are expansive, growing aspects of your well-being. Flexible and resilient, you bend and sway but don't break with the "weather" of circumstances. Caring for the tree of your well-being as you would a plant in your home, you water it, nourish it, smile at it, appreciate it, and learn to recognize what it needs. Decide that your tree is so important that it's not an option to wait until it's withering or injured to tend to it. Caring attentively to its varied

---

64   Nassim Nicholas Taleb, *Antifragile: Things that Gain from Disorder.*

aspects with compassion, your tree will thrive.

The practice of self-care includes getting to know what areas need more of your focus, and the best way to identify where you need to concentrate is by doing a whole-being scan. There are a myriad of examples of good self-care, but here I'll summarize the most important components from the roots up.

Roots

The roots of your tree support your conscious bravery, and the four essential elements are: *self-love;* union with the Divine, the universe, or *something greater;* your values and *beliefs;* and *support and connections* with others.

1. First, *self-love* nurtures your well-being and your whole being, motivating you to focus on the positives and choose things that serve you well. Committing to love yourself will prompt baby steps into self-care which will build over time. Your self-love will grow, and your motivation for self-care will increase because they fuel each other.

2. Second, staying connected to *what's greater,* you're rooted in trusting the process and can see past devastating circumstances. With these roots, you remember that "this too, shall pass," and live from love, meaning, and connection.

3. Third, *believing in* and living with optimism, you strengthen your foundation for bravery.

4. Fourth, *supporting others and receiving help,* you're stronger and never alone.

Spend time reflecting on where you need to place more energy to really strengthen your roots.

Trunk: Essence

Being in touch with your essence naturally prompts self-care. Your essence is like your trunk since it is the core of your being. Take time to meet with your essence on a daily basis, consciously breathing as you're one with your deepest self. You'll remember who you are when your circumstances question your very fiber. The bark of your tree connects you to your *self* and the world around you, just like your intuition. Learn to develop the ability to hear it and follow its direction. Your essence and intuition will tell you when you're due to make time for yourself.

Air: Presence

If you feel like you can't do anything else, come back into presence. The air of presence surrounds your tree. Returning to the now is the simplest self-care that's available any time, any place. It's free and takes only a second. Saturate yourself in this moment, and you'll feel restored. Practice breathing consciously and return to the now often. At the very least, you'll feel supported. Presence will uphold you.

Branches: Growth

Your branches are about how you keep growing. Each branch symbolizes an aspect of your health that needs regular attention. Become vibrant by developing all components of your well-being: physical, relational, work, financial, emotional, intellectual, spiritual, sexual, and service.

Physical—How you exist in your body is unique and broad-based. It has everything to do with how you maintain your heart and soul. Walk with grace and strength, your shoulders back, spine tall, heart open, poised and ready for anything, instead of hunching your shoulders as if you're carrying the burdens of the world. Lighten up and become a person who laughs more easily. Try this now: Prompt yourself by making a silly chuckle until it morphs into a genuine belly laugh. I do this with my sons and friends. It sparks joy. Other ways to take care of your body are: going to the doctor or dentist; showering or bathing daily; moving your body for at least thirty minutes three times a week—walking, doing yoga, Tai Chi, playing basketball, dancing, or doing *anything* you enjoy; getting a mani-pedi or a massage; eating healthy food; getting plenty of sleep; and drinking water.

You know what you need to do. *What will motivate you to do it?* Envision yourself feeling the way you want to feel. Commit to and schedule your self-care and/or get an accountability partner. Caring for your tall tree on a physical level brings you visceral pleasure.

Relational—Your relationships need your attentive care. For example, keeping healthy boundaries and using kind communication are essential with your addicted loved one. Boundaries are a form of self-care. My colleague Brad Reedy says you don't set boundaries to teach someone else a lesson or to change them; you set boundaries to take care of yourself.[65] Good boundaries help you respect both yourself and others.[66]

Work—All work is honorable when done with gratitude and wholeheartedness. Having a job you love is fulfilling, but try not to let work define you. It's wonderful to be passionate about what you do to make money, but balancing quality work with self-care keeps you energized and fresh, better able to serve and partner with your beloved. Collaborate when you can, and you are less likely to burn out. Teamwork with amazing, genuine humans is deliberate magic.

Financial—Your finances call out for your attention too. Don't spend beyond your means, and always put money into your savings. Some people view buying stuff as a reward, but it's a temporary fix. Caring for yourself by saving money is a more enduring satisfaction, and you'll learn to appreciate your prudent scrutiny by spending sensibly and saving consistently. Self-care in the financial and work arenas creates freedom through discipline.

Emotional—Befriend all your feelings and share them with your anam caras (soul friends). Allow yourself to do things that generate joy, such as connecting with friends, reflective journaling, taking yourself out for a meal or a mental health day, listening to music and making a new playlist with specific songs you love, or getting a hobby then sticking with it. Bring understanding to your situation, and do what you need to heal. You'll

---

65   Brad Reedy, *The Audacity to be You: Learning to Love Your Horrible, Rotten Self.*

66   Nedra Tawwab, *Set Boundaries, Find Peace: A Guide to Reclaiming Yourself.*

become more emotionally agile and spirited when you care for your heart, feeling flexible like a tree.

Intellectual—Stay sharp. Listen to podcasts, read, keep up with new information, and continue learning. Do puzzles, crosswords, or sudoku. Engage in open-minded, stimulating discussions. Find a topic that interests you and learn everything you can about it. Keep your brain stirred so that it doesn't feel the need to fixate on your loved one. When you need to make decisions on behalf of your beloved, your mind will be ready to engage with insight and can access wisdom.

Spiritual—Caring for your spirit is fulfilling. Let the light in by discovering what speaks to your soul, reaching your branches out to what brings you faith and hope. When you're close to the beauty of life in nature and art, the beauty you love will also be what you do.[67] Consider beginning and continuing a meditation practice, and you'll increase concentration, enhance awareness, lengthen your attention span, and clarify decision-making in addition to cultivating your spiritual foundation. Make time for solitude to hear your inner voice and boost your creativity.

Sexual—Sex is like a warm fire. Keep the coals burning often and your fire stays lit. A stress reducer and mood booster, remaining sexually active makes you feel more attractive and grounded. "What you don't use, you lose." Don't lose the potency of this magnetic, dynamic aspect of being human. There are great health benefits to sexual vibrancy, such as a robust immune system and heart, stroke, and cancer prevention, relief from headaches, and balanced hormones.[68]

Service—Service can lift you during difficult times. Volunteer if you can or do something as simple as washing the dishes at your friend's house after dinner. When you're helping others, good energy keeps flowing in and out.

---

67   Jalal al-din Rumi, *The Book of Love: Poems of Ecstasy and Longing*, translated by Coleman Barks.

68   Debra R. Wilson, PhD, "12 Ways Sex Helps You Live Longer." www.healthline.com.

Sunshine and Water

Trees need light and water to grow. Your tree is watered when you diligently utilize self-care for nurturing and revitalization. Do you truly want to be brave? Make regular time for self-care and you'll deepen your roots and expand branches for courage, daring, grace, and strength, reaching to the sun. Your tall tree will produce blossoms of satisfaction, and the fruit will be joy.

Empowered

By caring for your tree in its entirety, you're better prepared for anything that arises. Tending to all parts of your tree is easier than you may think. Start small with increased self-care in one area. It will fuel your motivation and empower you, increasing your happiness and vibrancy over time. With good self-care, new neuropathways in the brain are created, transforming into habits, and spurring on your antifragility. Best wishes as you begin!

BRAVERY KEY: SELF-CARE IS A FULFILLING AND NECESSARY LUXURY.

Practice self-care to further protect your happiness by structuring it into your life, and you'll bloom by living awake. Living awake from dawn till dark is the subject of the next chapter, and with the beginnings of compassionate self-care in place, peace and vitality will arise with greater ease.

CHAPTER 12

Live Awake from Dawn till Dark

"Stay close to anything that makes you glad you are alive."
—Hafiz

Living awake is conscious aliveness. Being in a conscious state of aliveness, living fully awake, is what I refer to as "awakeness" in this chapter. Imagine a resilient poppy in a spectacular field of orange wildflowers. Poppies are both strong and fragile, like humans, and grow in the most unlikely places, even desolate places.[69] Using the plant as an analogy, the roots of the poppy are your whole-being awareness. The green stem is your happiness, which you protect with your life. The colorful reddish-orange flower is the reward of the first two, the glorious beauty which blooms from your full awareness and happiness. With strong roots and a resilient stem, the flower blossoms brilliantly.

When deeply rooted in consciousness while protecting your contentment with everything you've got, you're not overwhelmed by the intensity of the fullness experienced on either end of the continuum from joy to pain. For example, hearing encouraging updates about your loved one's sobriety and mental health can induce fear about the future unless you are deeply rooted in awareness and have cultivated a solid foundation of happiness. Or, if a friend of your beloved's overdoses or takes their own life, you might feel crushed that their precious life ended. Being sensitive and vulnerable, the end of a life can knock you down, but with awareness and happiness to

---

69   "History of the Memorial Day Poppy Flower Symbol," from www.goodhousekeeping. com.

return to, you will manage the dark along with the light that living awake brings.

"Awake" means different things in different circles. Here, by awake I mean intentional fullness, a richness that is the fruit of engaged awareness and resilient happiness! You live awakened, with inspired vibrancy, robustness, and spunk. By manifesting this energetic vitality, you no longer have to merely *exist* in a dulled and saddened life, simply getting by, easily swayed by circumstances.

It can feel risky to live awake, especially when allowing more joy also means capacity to feel greater pain. However, it is necessary to abandon old and worn-out ways of hovering above your life instead of fully touching down, as these no longer serve you. Doing anything less will prevent you from living your bliss. You deserve a life of joy. A life you love. By making a covenant with yourself to become braver, you diligently combine and integrate concepts and strategies that keep you close to your instinctive aliveness. It actually takes bravery to cultivate happiness and live fully awake.

Now we'll dive into the essential props needed to deliberately *hold up your awakeness:* finding meaning, trusting the process, nature, creativity, humor and play, and sensory awakening.

Finding Meaning

It's easy to live *for* other people at times, especially when your loved ones have tremendous and frequent hardships. Discovering deeper significance gives me purpose and optimism. I find meaning from the strong force of courageous love because I love my sons and life itself. I refuse to let addiction hardships destroy my unconditional love for who they truly are. I refuse to let anything interfere with that or my true happiness and joy in life. Brave love is an inspiring purpose.

Discover what truly makes you excited or able to get out of bed every morning, regardless of circumstances. This will help you find your personal meaning. Intimately linked with inner purpose, you become more confident in decisions surrounding your loved ones and their complex worlds. Living with a mission emerging from clearly defined meaning gives you gumption to return to bravery, over and over and over again. Don't just search for meaning, find it. Ask yourself questions, then reflect to uncover deeply motivating answers. For example, ask "What is your destiny as you understand it here and now?" Refrain from limiting yourself to thinking about the fires you need to put out. Stir up the coals that will reignite your inner fire. What are you living for? What provides meaning for you? What is your purpose now? What is your life's purpose? What brings renewal and healing? What do *you* need in order to live a life you love? Your answers may change, but wrestling with and answering these questions continuously is essential to living awake.

Trusting the Process

When you trust the process, you're trusting both something greater than you, and yourself. Knowing you can only control *you*, you're not attached to a particular outcome, with radical faith that circumstances will ultimately find some resolution in their own time. If you're not willing to completely trust the process, you're susceptible to desperation, angst, fear, and hopelessness. With faith, you deliberately abandon old ways, understanding that things may be difficult now, but they will change and likely improve. As with assertive surrender, it may feel reckless to bow to fate and comfort yourself. Yet knowing that what you've already been through—devastating as it was—you are here now in a new place. It may even be an exciting, happier place, as you're blooming in your true essence. Try something with me: Walk around as you read, and say this aloud: *I trust the flow. Walking my own authentic path, I do what I can. I choose to let go of the rest.*[70] When you commit to the need for fierce trust, you reset into it repeatedly. Our universe is infinite and mysterious. Will you choose to consciously trust its wisdom, with its give and take, ups and downs?

---

70   Tad Schexnailder, DC Organic Living Chiropractic. Tad practices sensory awareness during network spinal treatments with patients. He has postdoctoral training in Addictionology, among other specialties, and we've had a hundred stimulating discussions.

Nature

Because happiness is your foundation and gratitude maintains it, you're walking with infinite power. Being outside in nature reinforces this and brings reprieve and relief. Nature connects you with beauty and sparks your whole being in liveliness. Making a change in your environment is a reviving energy shift. Just going outside in the *fresh air* for fifteen minutes during your day alters your perspective and makes you feel fresh, whether it's sunny or cloudy, warm or cold. You bravely risk turning up the pleasure dial as all of your senses take in the natural world and you reawaken!

Longer periods of rejuvenation in nature stimulate even greater healing: hiking, biking, climbing, kayaking, swimming, bathing in a hot spring, gazing at the ocean, sitting on a parking bench, lying in a hammock, doing yoga, meditating, enjoying an outdoor concert, creating, singing, making music, or any form of modified *movement*. Doing anything you love that is satisfying rejuvenates your whole being, and you can usually find a way to do it outside. Even if your circumstances are limited and you cannot get out in nature, you can always close your eyes and imagine it. Try it now by imagining bright, warm sunshine on your face. Then envision bright stars glistening outside in the dark.

Why outside; what is the power there? Nature is sentient. It's alive, awake, vibrating with color, movement, sound, and potential. When you're in it, you're one with it, and you're imparted with its powerful influence. Nature is active; it's always changing. If you don't know the healing power of being in nature, give it a try for one week. Immersion in nature reduces blood pressure, tension and anxiety, boosts your immune system, and produces all kinds of cardiovascular, metabolic, and dopamine enhancement.[71] I've gone on walks where my goal is simply to take in all the variations of green. Focusing on that, my mind is eased and my whole being wakes up with energized life. I immediately feel the soothing force of connection to the world around me, linking with the immense cosmos! The sun, moon, and stars can remind you that you are supported by a beautiful universe. Stars

---

71   "The Art and Science of Forest Bathing," www.adventuresnw.com.

connect you with the infinite, because the ones you're seeing are already gone. It's mind boggling, waking you up into a more spacious perspective!

Creativity

Sometimes words cannot adequately articulate what you feel, and it has to be expressed in another form. Tap into the realm of imagination, which has no bounds. That's part of what makes it so freeing. There are no restrictions with creativity! You're "loos'd of limits and imaginary lines."[72] Deriving pleasure from creating something is not only going to make you feel better, you'll also be liberated.[73]

The source of creativity is divine, connecting you with golden threads to the mystical realms of music, art, and invention. Everyone is creative in different ways, because creativity is your soul's voice and is "coaxed by treats like permission and acceptance."[74] Creativity is a massive dynamo that needs space to evolve; give it an honorable seat in your world. Tending to your creative fire is a discipline of self-fulfillment.[75] It's best not to analyze what pleases you; you must just do it.

Using Humor and Play Brain

Humor through comic relief keeps you rising amidst it all. Parents and loved ones of people suffering from substance use or emotional problems can easily look on the dark side, making it hard to keep the faith at times. Bringing lightness to the heaviness you sustain yourself, and your bravery endures through all things. Conjure up your inner Chandler Bing from the television show "Friends," by just being playful or silly, and find some relief in a comical sense.[76] Let yourself laugh and smile more often. Giving yourself permission to be lighthearted lifts you into a more awake state, altering the brain, helping you think better.

---

72   Walt Whitman, "Song of the Open Road, 5."

73   Elizabeth Gilbert, "Magic Lessons" podcast.

74   Michelle Waters is one of the most creative leaders and trainers I know. See her blogspot, "53 Things I Think I Know" with numbered "head tilts," as she tilts her "head to the side to see what comes out."

75   Clarissa Pinkola Estés, PhD, "Your Creative Fire" audible, www.soundstrue.com.

76   Matthew Perry's character from TV sitcom, Friends.

There's a reason that even dramatic films and TV shows incorporate comic relief. In *Star Wars*, there are the Ewoks and droids, delivering lines to make us laugh just when we need a reprieve from the heaviness of a scene. Even Han Solo breaks it up by punctuating scenes with a line like, "I've got a bad feeling about this." I call this "play brain."[77] When you intentionally "lighten up" in life, without a script the brain attempts to bring playful or lighthearted relief to the intensity of a situation. Ignite your creative fuel with *"play brain,"* spontaneously or via a structured event in your week, like trivia night. Anything that helps you press pause on intensity creates a shift in your day into awakeness. Break up hours with moments of *play* here and there. You stimulate your brain and body when playing an instrument, painting, snapping a photo, solving puzzles, or playing at food creations. Anything creative engages your "play brain," body, and heart in new and different ways, making you more efficient and capable of being present with your loved ones.

Sensory Awakening

It's a few years back, and I'm in the rain forest on the Big Island of Hawaii with friends. A whirlwind of chaos is going on at home, and it was hard for me to leave, but the vacation had been planned for a long time. Walking on retreat together through the enchanting Kona Cloud Forest, we're listening to Mariah, our native Hawaiian way finder,[78] and we are alone. She's taking us on a Wild Awakening Experience, explaining how to broaden our peripheral vision. We're told to be wide-eyed like owls as we turn our heads slowly from side to side, taking in everything around us. I extend both arms straight out horizontally on either side of myself, still able to see my hands. Switching, I extend one up vertically and the other straight down to the ground, seeing the oval span of my visual field. That is

---

77   Derek Campbell originally coined the phrase.

78   Mariah Mann is a trained way finder, a naturalist who is deeply connected to nature. She was mentored by respected elders, received training on Kauai and in Canada, and has studied and lived in eight different countries. I highly recommend the magic she brings: www.journeysinthenaau.com.

my "owl-seeing" view. She then instructs us to "pretend play" and imagine that we're foxes walking leisurely and quietly with curiosity, responding instinctually as we notice everything around us. Feeling my skin and bones with bare feet on the brown dirt and twigs of the forest floor, I sharpen my hearing and stroll forward like an ambling fox, watching and perceiving the environment like an owl, paying attention to details close by, in addition to movement and sounds far away. We move with "fox-walking and owl-seeing," simultaneously with microscopic precision and zoom-lens vision, pretending that we are wild, and this forest is our domain. The dial for every sense I have is turned up to its maximum capacity, and I feel the living current. It's an awakening. And it's wild.

When we smile at one another, we've been slightly transformed, and gratitude emanates between us. This exchange with my friends sustains me later when I call my sons on the phone and hold space for them in dealing with their struggles. I no longer let my loved ones' situations put me in a box of fear or anxiety, or believe I am unable to lead a life with some happiness on vacation. I don't feel as burdened and can offer encouragement, because I just took in something rich that enlightened me to awaken and trust in the process. Protecting my happiness, I hold all of it together, the pain my sons are going through along with the joy I just experienced.

Paying attention to everything I can with conscious, heightened senses from my entire being has repeatedly pulled me out of a place of discouragement regarding the parts of my life that can so easily drag me down. Living in a constant state of awakeness has instinctually helped me remember that the chaos going on within my family doesn't have the power to stop me from loving other parts of life and finding joy in moments of happiness. This practice of "fox-walking" and "owl-seeing" isn't just a fun thing to do in a rainforest on retreat; it's a technique for waking up that you can take consciously into hardships to help you compartmentalize, separating out what's troubling you from how beautiful each moment is. You're not discounting your pain; you're saturating yourself with what's in front of you. Choosing to live harmoniously with two things that are true at once, you focus on the pleasant experience just for the time being. You know you'll come back to tend to your discomfort, but for now you allow yourself the delight of a beautiful experience.

Try it right now if you can. Wherever you are, extend both arms out wide, then vertically, viewing your hands to see the extent of your peripheral vision. Now walk around for one minute with heightened sensory awareness, both a "fox-walking" body and "owl-seeing" eyes, fully engaging your intuition and energy. You are consciously awake, observing everything, and there is no "story" in your mind about what you're witnessing. If you can, get down on all fours like a fox. Watch, feel, and listen with keen awareness, observing things from the broadest peripheral vision available along with the greatest attention to detail. Stand back up. In a full-on immersive experience, you're standing on your foundation of happiness, feeling the strength in your bones and the lightness in your heart.

A wild awakening occurs within you whenever you tap into your instincts, vibrantly and fully alive in as many moments possible. Anchored from true happiness and with awareness, you have everything you need to "walk your walk" into bravery, deliberately living awake from dawn till dark. Imagine doing this when you're down or worried and want to remember how to manifest a new way of life, consciously awake. Prepare and train by *integrating* the happiness and living-awake practices here. They'll become embedded in both your brain and your habits. You'll use them instinctually when needed, even during a crisis. Growing capacity to experience deeper awakeness for longer periods of time sparks bliss.[79] Whatever excites you, whatever makes you feel brighter and more vibrant, those are what you need to do daily. You're alive. Live it consciously awake.

BRAVERY KEY: WHAT IS NECESSARY IS A SORT OF DELIBERATE YET RECKLESS ABANDONMENT OF OLD WAYS, PARTNERED WITH RADICAL FAITH IN A NEW WAY OF LIFE WITH CONSCIOUS AWAKENING.

All the concepts thus far provide a foundation for bravery. You understand

---

79   Bonnie Badenoch, *Being a Brain-Wise Therapist*. The phrase "spark joy" was coined by Marie Kondo in her book, *Spark Joy*.

the basics. Conscious bravery only becomes ingrained when you *practice* it, in both the easier moments and the difficult times. *Integrate* these concepts into your life and use them with awareness daily. Transformation happens in moments. You will begin to transform. You are the best person to bring the faith, hope, and bravery you need into your life. Do something small every day, and you'll live with the awakened fullness you long for.

You've begun focused work in conscious bravery, and I respect you. We are walking alongside, together, here. Arm in arm, as you continue in your efforts, remember that you have what you need to keep going. I am with you, along with our tribe of other parents and loved ones in this addiction and mental health realm. You're never alone and are braver than you know.

Closing

Walk this path with gentleness, lightness, and focused hope. Keep faith burning inside you, overriding regrets, dear one. Lean into what you must do with less fear. A lot of how you'll thrive in the wilderness will come down to not just how you frame things in your mind, but your choices and the actions you take. You've already come a long way! You picked up this book and are integrating the concepts. Give yourself credit for what you have done thus far. You want to be more brave and are taking the steps you can. I'm grateful and honored you've chosen to partner with me and respect you in all of your efforts.

What will motivate you to keep going? Find that answer for yourself and anchor securely in it. For me, it's love. Love is the answer to almost every question. Love keeps me going, for myself and my sons. How can you love more? Tap into any self-love you do have and be gentle with yourself as you go. Your love will grow. Love with such great commitment and gracious tenacity that the insights into bravery you long for emerge. The awareness and energy you need for courageous actions will be there, blooming from love.

I feel with you deeply in your pain and all the adversity you've been through. I'm here with you, amid the harsh terrain on the very same undesired, unexplored trail in the wilderness. You're not alone. None of us are ever alone. We are one, and we are here together, you and I. Many who love someone touched by addiction are out here with us, and some have found their way into peace. Arm in arm, we are a tribe of supporters who lean on one another to solidify our path into awakening and joy.

You're giving yourself a gift by listening to your own deep wisdom from within, to access your bravery. What you come to know will matter even more over time. Whatever ounce of bravery you can muster is enough for that day. Let go of self-induced pressure. Being present while in this unremitting territory is hard enough. When you commit to love and bravely put that love into action, you'll continue to do what it takes. Cultivating your unique style is *your own truest bravery*.

Your conscious bravery will bring you relief and joy. You are awake and alive. Remember who you are. You are more than the "me" you are today, and who you are today is already enough.

Keep journeying and protect your happiness and vibrancy. May you have many fully present moments!

Be brave.

With love, Pamela

Next Steps

If you want to deepen your conscious bravery, you can go to my website, www.BeBrave.us. It offers blogs, techniques, tools, and practices for further support and guidance into courage and awareness. There, I'll post information about my upcoming book, podcast appearances, and live sessions.

Also, see info and continued posts on: Facebook: Pamela Brinker, Author; on Instagram: bebravewithpamelabrinker; and on LinkedIn: Pamela Brinker, LCSW.

Resources List

For You: Resources for Those Who Love Someone with Addiction

Adult Children of Alcoholics (ACA) (adultchildren.org)

Al-Anon (al-anon.org)

Changes Parent Support Network (cpsn.org; national)

CoDA, (CoDA.org)

CRAFT Method (helpingfamilies.help.com)

Families Anonymous (familiesanonymous.org)

Nar-Anon (nar-anon.org)

S-Anon (sanon.org)

Springs Recovery Connection (srchope.org; local to Colorado).

Addiction and Mental Health Resources

LEAP Institute (LEAPInstitute.org)

NAMI (National Alliance for Mental Illness)

VeryWellMind.com

For Your Loved One: Support for those with Addictions

Alcoholics Anonymous (AA) (aa.org)

All Addictions Anonymous (alladdictionsanonymous.org)

Cocaine Anonymous (CA) (ca.org)

Crystal Meth Anonymous (CMA) (crystalmeth.org)

Dual Recovery Anonymous (UK) (dualrecoveryanonymous.org)

Food Addicts in Recovery Anonymous (FA) (foodaddicts.org)

Gamblers Anonymous (GA) (gamblersanonymous.org)

Marijuana Anonymous (marijuana-anonymous.org)

Methadone Anonymous (methadonesupport.org)

Narcotics Anonymous (NA) (na.org)

Nicotine Anonymous (nicotine-anonymous.org)

Recovery Dharma (recoverydharma.org)

Recovery Diaries (oc87recoverydiaries.org)

Sex and Love Addicts Anonymous (SLAA) (slaafws.org)

Sexaholics Anonymous (sa.org)

SMART Recovery (smartrecovery.org)

Women for Sobriety (WFS) (womenforsobroety.org)

XA Speakers (xa-speakers.org)

Yoga of 12-Step Recovery (y12sr.com)

Online Self-Help Forums for Addicts

AA Intergroup (aa-intergroup.org)

Addiction Recovery Guide (addictionrecoveryguide.org)

Addiction Survivors (addictionsurvivors.org)

NA Chat (na-chat.com)

Soberistas (soberistas.com)

Support Groups (supportgroups.com)

12-Step Forums (12stepforums.net)

Treatment Locator

Substance Abuse Treatment Facility Locator for US (findtreatment.samhsa.gov)

Recovery: www.recovery.org

About the Author

Pamela W. Brinker holds a master's degree in social work from the University of Denver and has been a licensed clinical psychotherapist in private practice for over twenty years. She has guided clients on their journeys through pain into bravery, and leads workshops and trainings in this arena. She provides direction and healing to those attempting to manage their lives while they assist loved ones who suffer with addictions and mental health issues. As a passionate therapist, speaker, educator, and advocate for personal growth and mental health awareness, Pamela has created her own valuable techniques and tools to cultivate courage and find more freedom. She is married and has two sons and a stepson. She loves the mountains as well as the ocean, and resides in Colorado where she enjoys practicing yoga, skate skiing, hiking, cycling, poetry, reading and writing, as well as playing her ukulele or piano and singing.

Pamela can be contacted for information and media appearances at www.bebrave.us She can also be found sharing messages of courage, hope, and bravery at the following locations:

Instagram: bebravewithpamelabrinker

Facebook: Pamela Brinker, Author

LinkedIn: Pamela Brinker, LCSW

YouTube: BeBrave by Pamela Brinker